~ UNIVERSAL MYTHS ~

WARRING GODS

IMMORTAL BATTLE MYTHS
AROUND THE WORLD

Graphic Library is published by Capstone Press,
1710 Roe Crest Drive, North Mankato, Minnesota 56003
www.mycapstone.com

Library of Congress Cataloging-in-Publication data is available on the Library of Congress website.
ISBN 978-1-5157-6628-5 (library binding)
ISBN 978-1-5157-6632-2 (paperback)
ISBN 978-1-5157-6636-0 (eBook PDF)

Summary: Read tales of godly fights and wars in seven battle myths from various mythologies and traditions around the world — all told in gripping graphic novel format.

Editor
Abby Huff

Art Director
Nathan Gassman

Designer
Ted Williams

Media Researcher
Jo Miller

Production Specialist
Kathy McColley

Inker and Colorist
Eduardo Garcia

Thanks to our consultant Daniel Peretti, PhD, for lending his expertise and advice.

Design Element: Shutterstock: dalmingo (map),
ilolab, maradon 333, Milos Djapovic, NuConcept Dezine

Printed in the United States 4651

TABLE OF CONTENTS

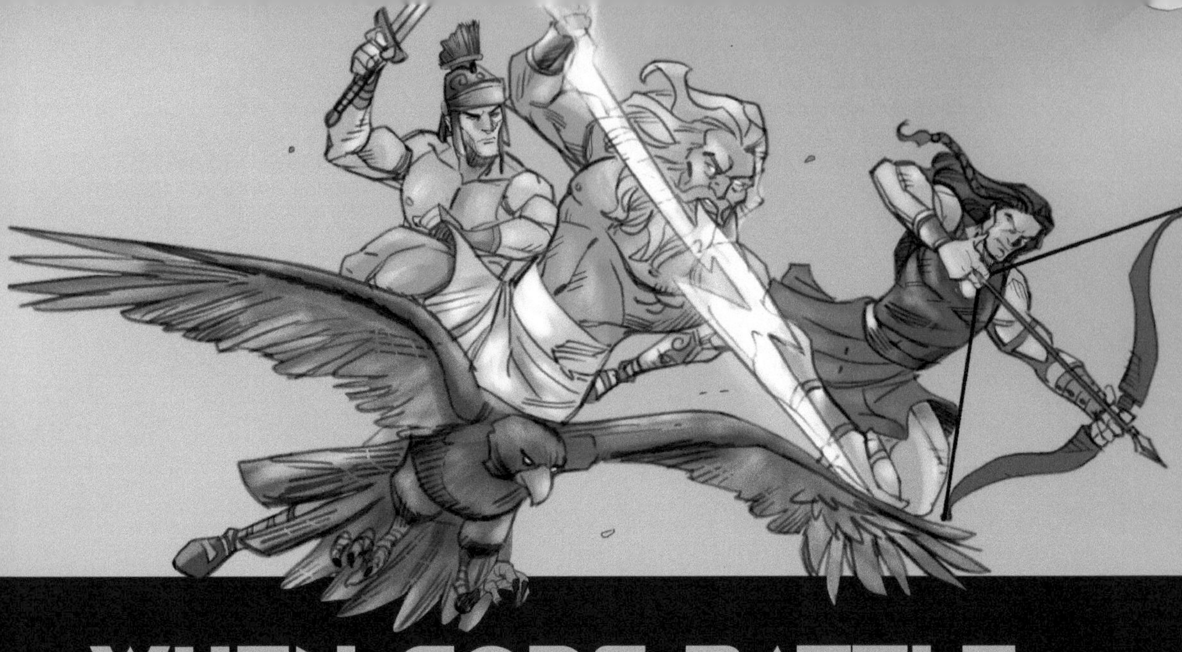

WHEN GODS BATTLE

In the distance, a flash of light splits the clouds. Seconds later, deep rumbling shakes the earth. To ancient peoples, bolts of lightning and booming thunder sometimes signaled more than an approaching storm. They believed that high in the heavens, great armies of gods could be waging war for control of the universe — the clash of their swords and the thunder of their collisions lighting up the night sky. It's just one of countless old myths about gods battling gods.

A myth is a story that explains a culture's connection to its past and its relationship with the world. Most cultures throughout the world have some form of mythology, or a collection of myths. In ancient societies, myths helped describe how life began, the origin of the sun and the moon, the forces of good and evil, and many other mysteries of life itself.

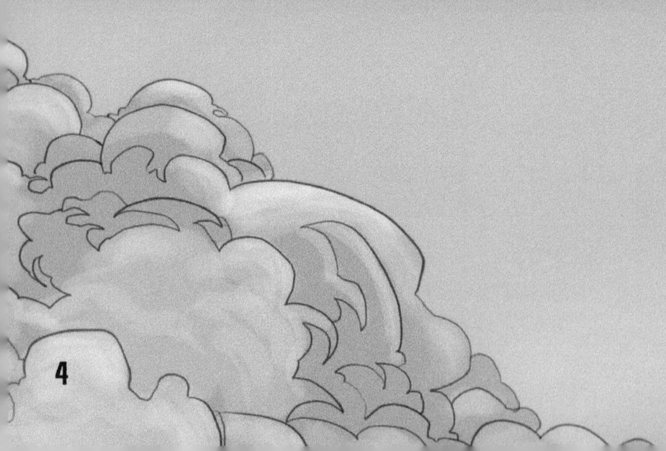

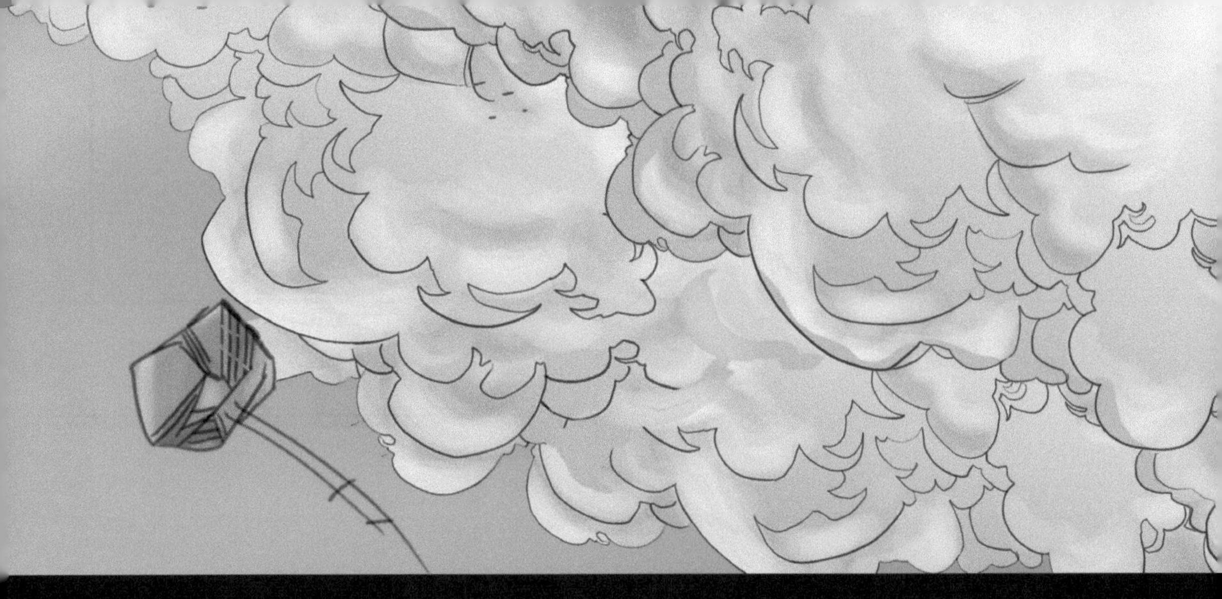

Fighting between gods and goddesses has long been part of many cultures' mythologies. Battle myths, or combat myths, frequently describe supernatural struggles for power between good and evil, or order and chaos. Often these stories begin with a serious threat to the gods. The danger usually comes either from within the pantheon of gods or from an outside force. The gods that represent good war against an enemy that represents wickedness or disorder. The defeat of evil and return to order is an important theme throughout the myths.

Handed down from generation to generation, battle myths showed ancient peoples which qualities their community valued. The stories that follow emphasize that courage, loyalty, and obedience to the law are essential for thriving societies — a lesson that has endured for thousands of years.

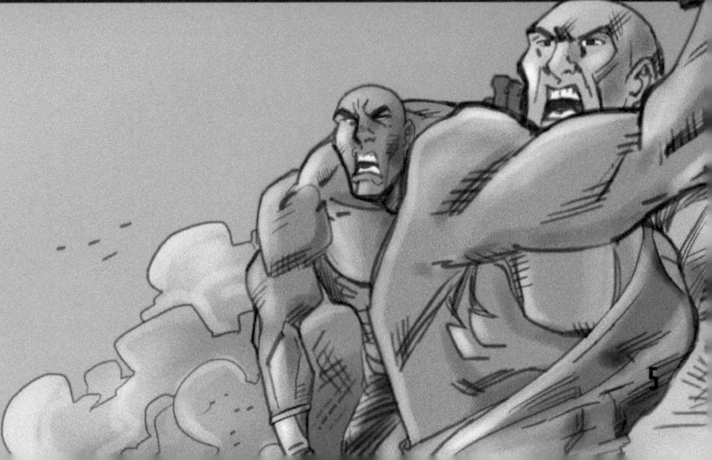

CHAPTER ONE

THE WAR OF THE TITANS

A GREEK MYTH

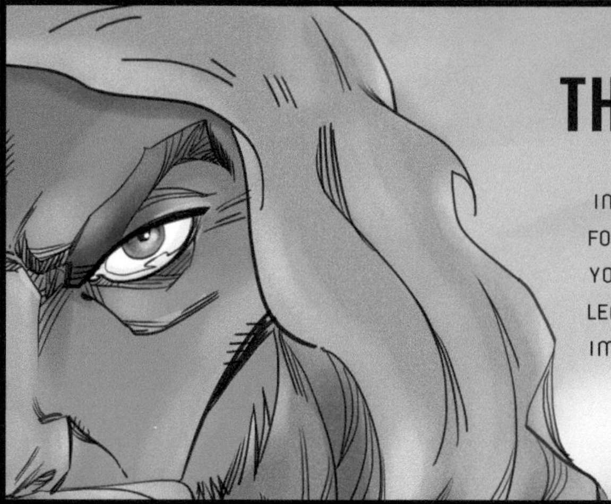

IN ANCIENT GREEK MYTHOLOGY, A GREAT WAR WAS FOUGHT BETWEEN THE TITANS, THE FIRST GODS, AND YOUNGER GODS CALLED THE OLYMPIANS. WITH ZEUS LEADING THE OLYMPIANS, THE BATTLE BETWEEN THE IMMORTALS RAGED ON FOR TEN YEARS. THE RESULT OF THE WAR WOULD DETERMINE WHICH GROUP WOULD BECOME RULERS OF ALL.

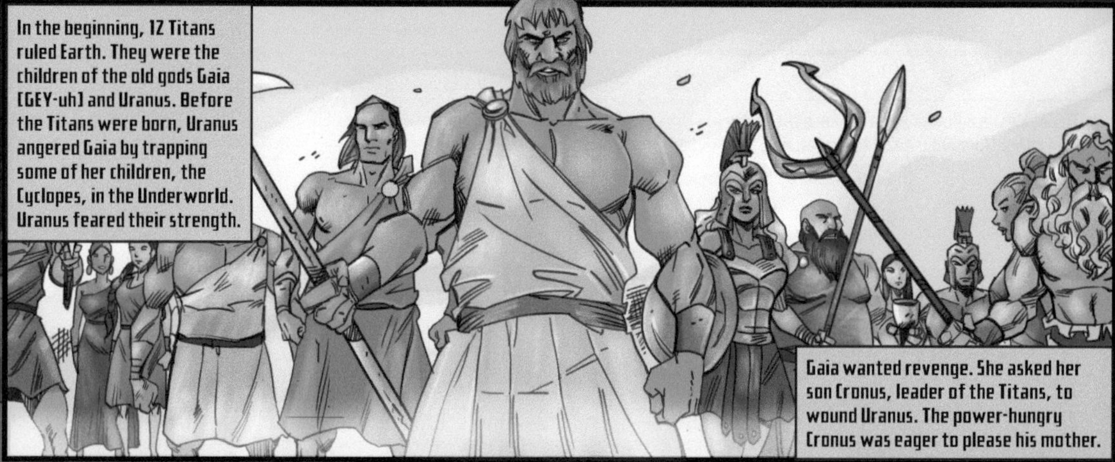
In the beginning, 12 Titans ruled Earth. They were the children of the old gods Gaia [GEY-uh] and Uranus. Before the Titans were born, Uranus angered Gaia by trapping some of her children, the Cyclopes, in the Underworld. Uranus feared their strength.
Gaia wanted revenge. She asked her son Cronus, leader of the Titans, to wound Uranus. The power-hungry Cronus was eager to please his mother.

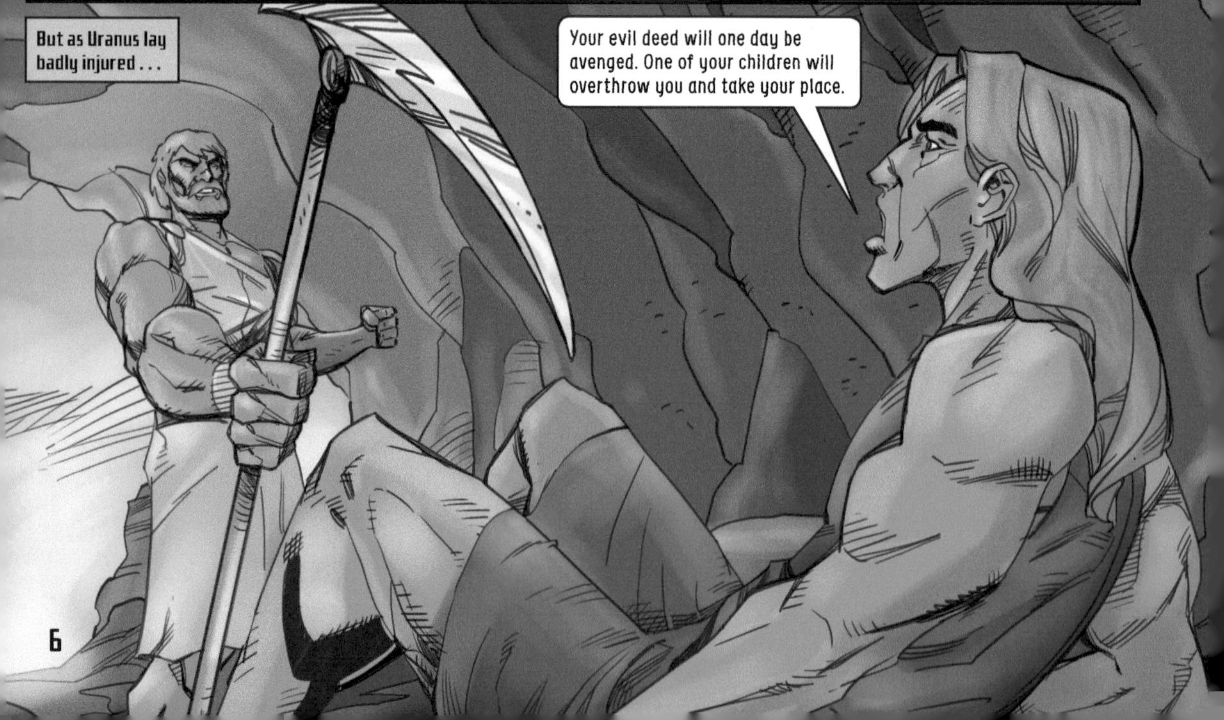
But as Uranus lay badly injured . . .
Your evil deed will one day be avenged. One of your children will overthrow you and take your place.

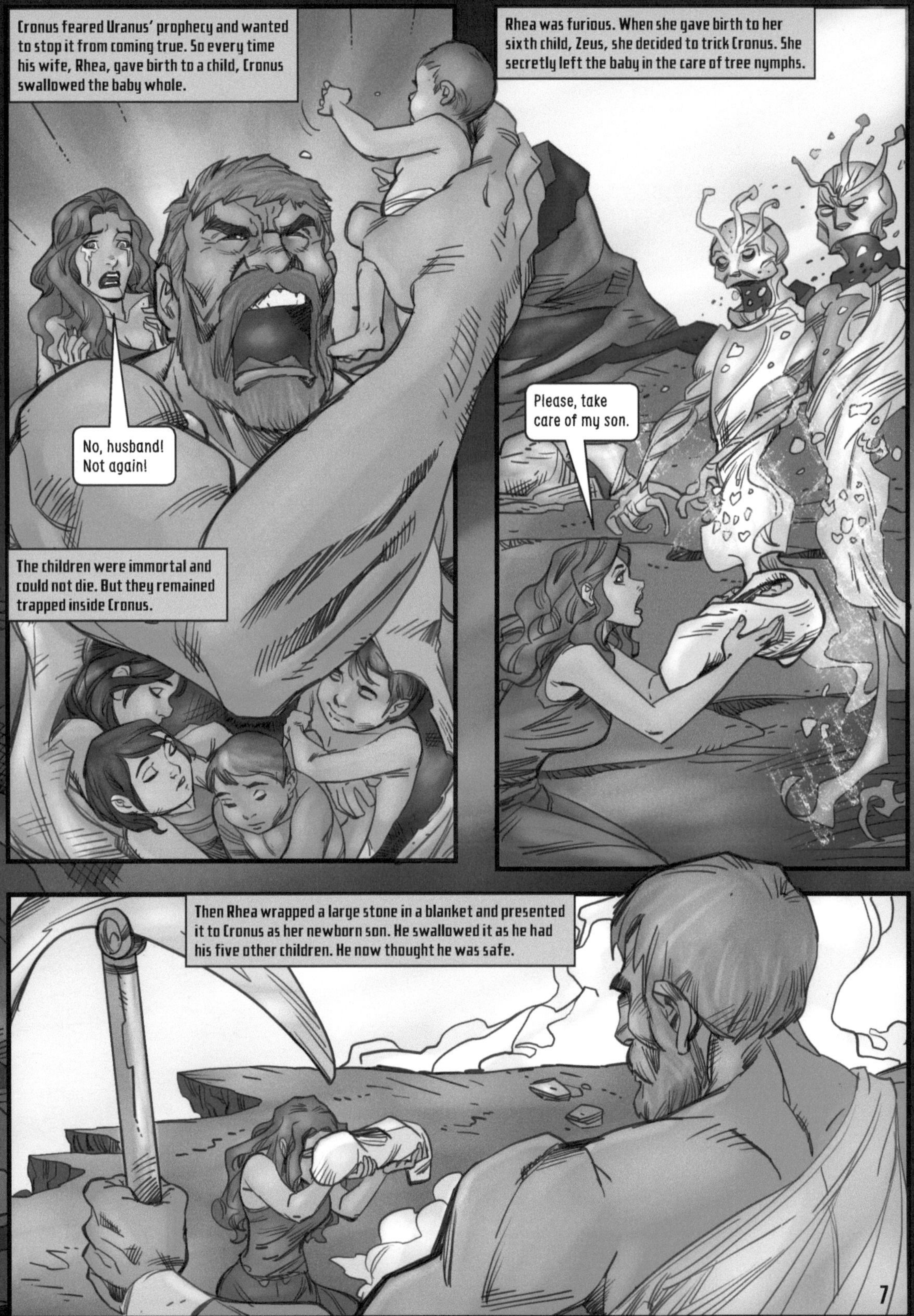

Cronus feared Uranus' prophecy and wanted to stop it from coming true. So every time his wife, Rhea, gave birth to a child, Cronus swallowed the baby whole.
No, husband! Not again!
The children were immortal and could not die. But they remained trapped inside Cronus.
Rhea was furious. When she gave birth to her sixth child, Zeus, she decided to trick Cronus. She secretly left the baby in the care of tree nymphs.
Please, take care of my son.
Then Rhea wrapped a large stone in a blanket and presented it to Cronus as her newborn son. He swallowed it as he had his five other children. He now thought he was safe.

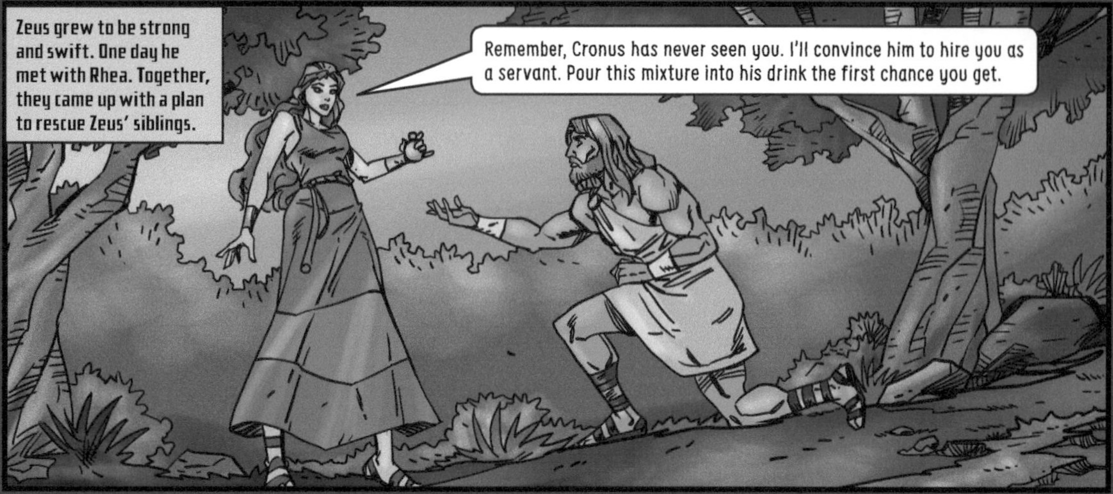
Zeus grew to be strong and swift. One day he met with Rhea. Together, they came up with a plan to rescue Zeus' siblings.
Remember, Cronus has never seen you. I'll convince him to hire you as a servant. Pour this mixture into his drink the first chance you get.

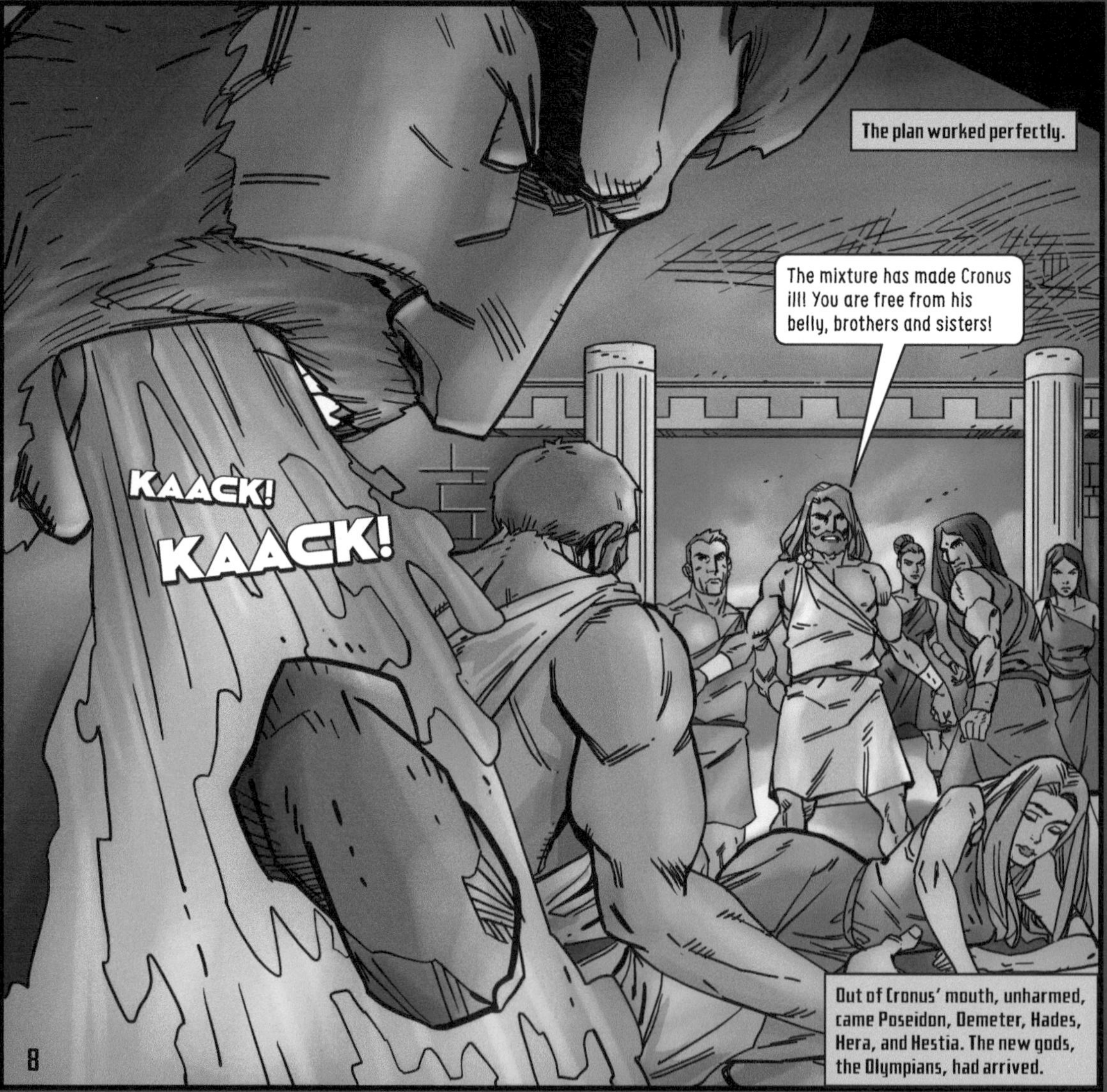
The plan worked perfectly.
KAACK!
KAACK!
The mixture has made Cronus ill! You are free from his belly, brothers and sisters!
Out of Cronus' mouth, unharmed, came Poseidon, Demeter, Hades, Hera, and Hestia. The new gods, the Olympians, had arrived.

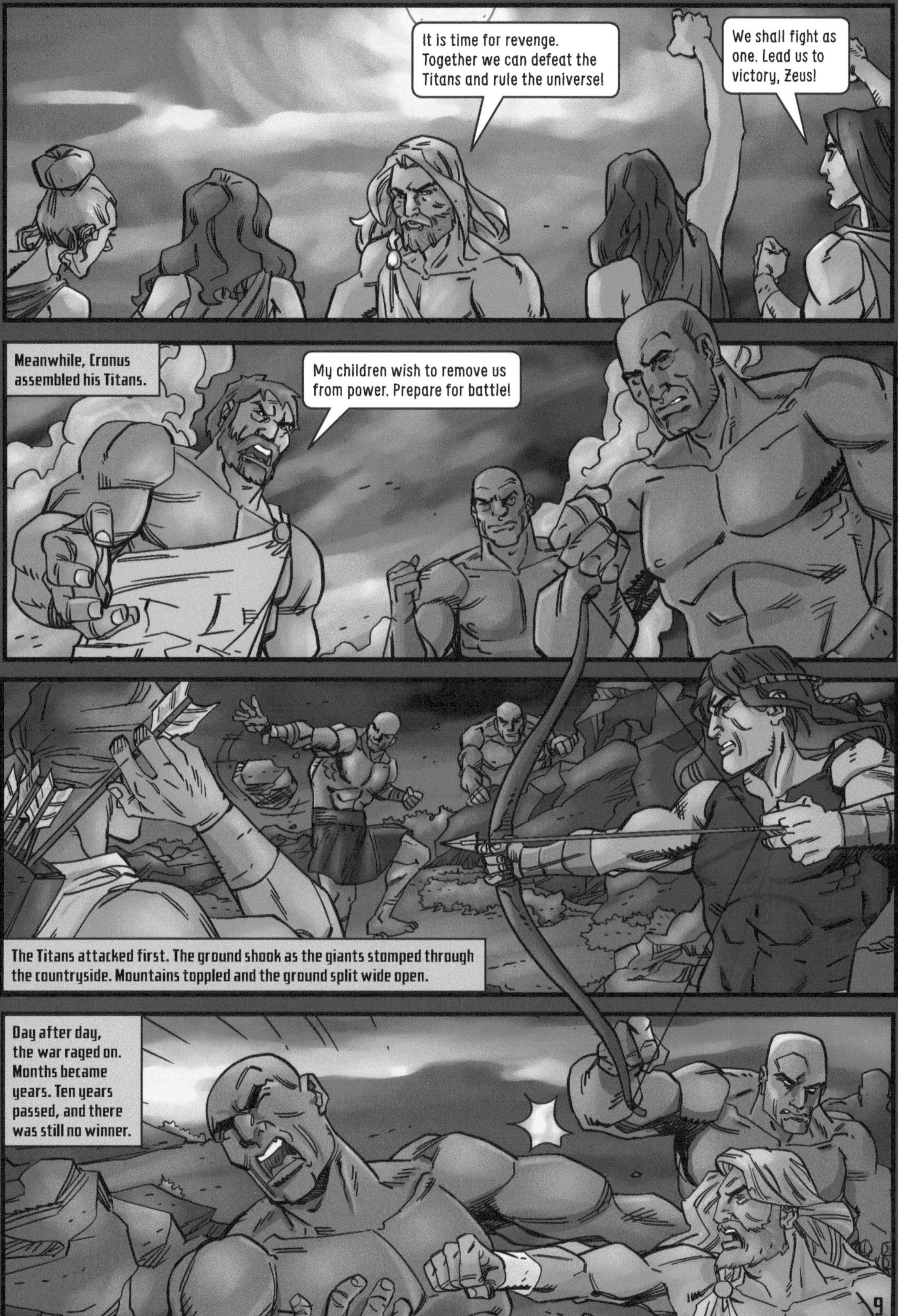
It is time for revenge. Together we can defeat the Titans and rule the universe!
We shall fight as one. Lead us to victory, Zeus!
Meanwhile, Cronus assembled his Titans.
My children wish to remove us from power. Prepare for battle!
The Titans attacked first. The ground shook as the giants stomped through the countryside. Mountains toppled and the ground split wide open.
Day after day, the war raged on. Months became years. Ten years passed, and there was still no winner.

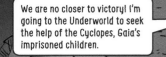

We are no closer to victory! I'm going to the Underworld to seek the help of the Cyclopes, Gaia's imprisoned children.

We pray for your safe return.

Soon . . .

Cyclopes! I am your nephew Zeus. Your brother Cronus has kept you locked away for too long. I will set you free if you fight on my side.

We will fight with you, Zeus. And we will make strong weapons for you — thunderbolts and a trident!

Zeus returned to the world above with his allies, more powerful than ever. The Olympians attacked the Titans with new strength.

After many battles, the Olympians defeated the Titans and imprisoned them in the Underworld.

Grateful for their freedom, the Cyclopes built the Olympians a magnificent palace on top of Mount Olympus.

There the Olympians took their place as the new gods. With Zeus as their leader, they became rulers of the universe.

DID YOU KNOW?

In the second and first centuries BC, the Romans defeated the Greek empire. The Greek civilization was a source of inspiration to the Romans. Much of Roman mythology is based on Greek myths, but the gods have simply been renamed. For example, Greece's Poseidon and Rome's Neptune are both gods of the sea. The Greek Zeus and the Roman Jupiter both command their groups of gods.

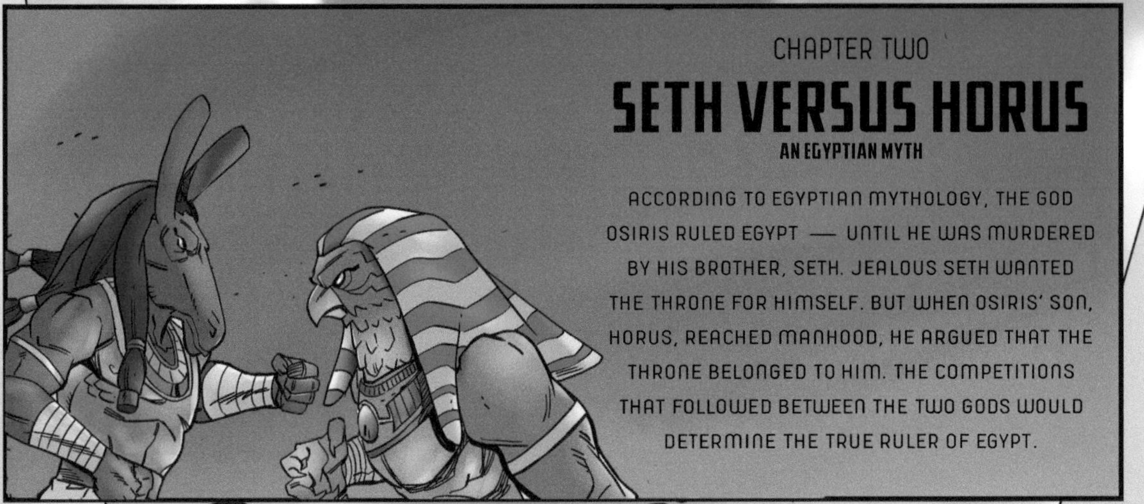
CHAPTER TWO
SETH VERSUS HORUS
AN EGYPTIAN MYTH
ACCORDING TO EGYPTIAN MYTHOLOGY, THE GOD OSIRIS RULED EGYPT — UNTIL HE WAS MURDERED BY HIS BROTHER, SETH. JEALOUS SETH WANTED THE THRONE FOR HIMSELF. BUT WHEN OSIRIS' SON, HORUS, REACHED MANHOOD, HE ARGUED THAT THE THRONE BELONGED TO HIM. THE COMPETITIONS THAT FOLLOWED BETWEEN THE TWO GODS WOULD DETERMINE THE TRUE RULER OF EGYPT.

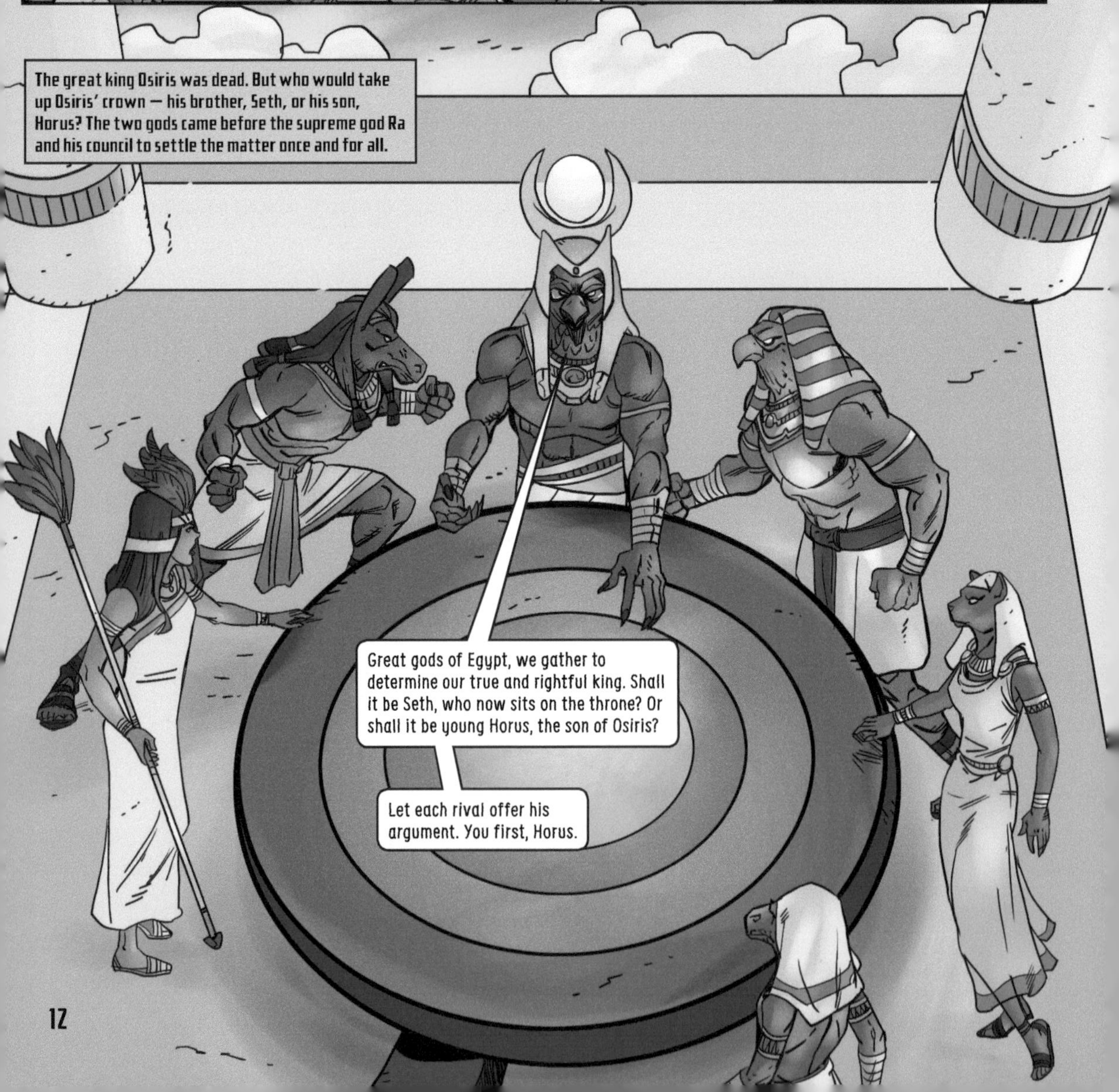
The great king Osiris was dead. But who would take up Osiris' crown — his brother, Seth, or his son, Horus? The two gods came before the supreme god Ra and his council to settle the matter once and for all.
Great gods of Egypt, we gather to determine our true and rightful king. Shall it be Seth, who now sits on the throne? Or shall it be young Horus, the son of Osiris?
Let each rival offer his argument. You first, Horus.

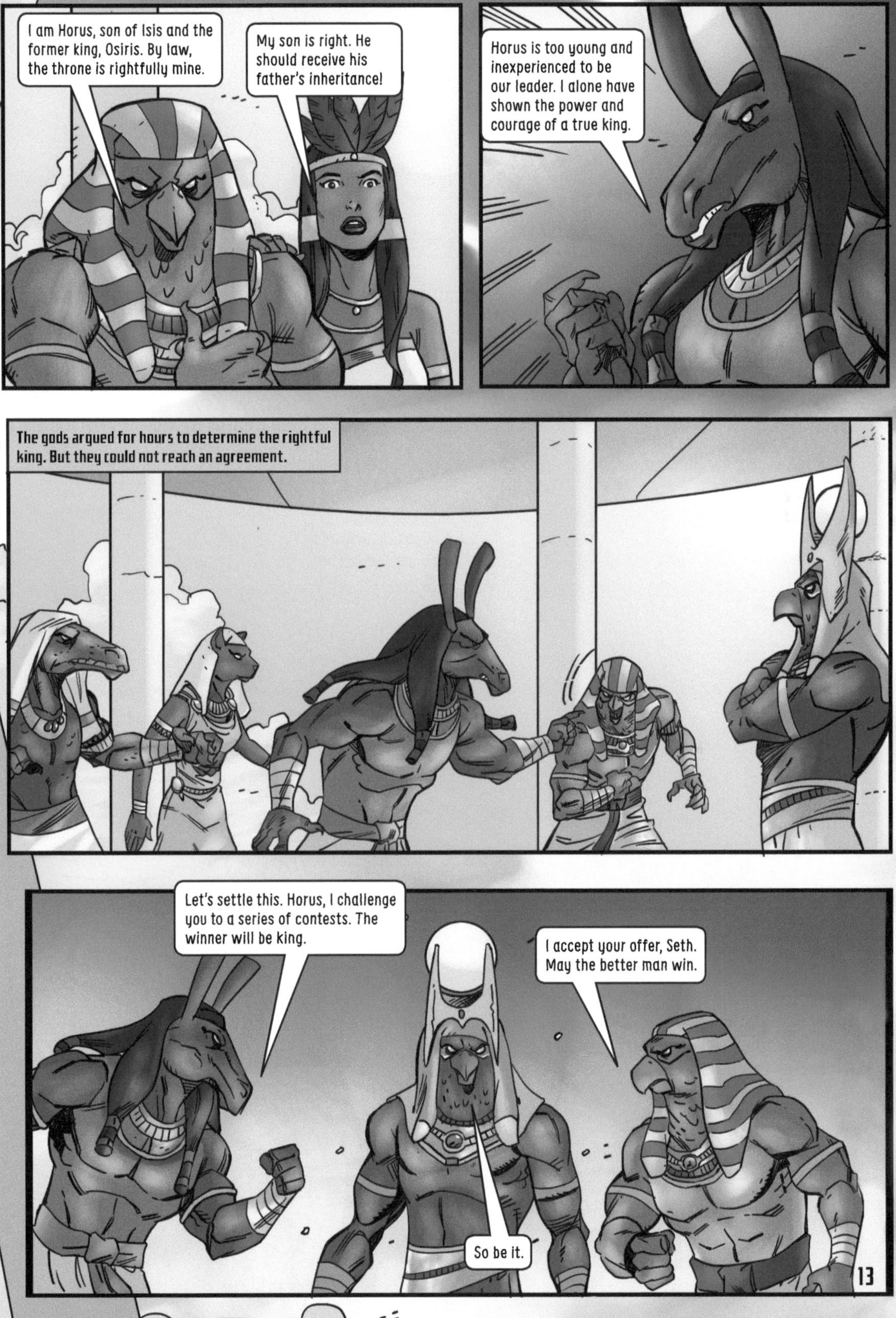
I am Horus, son of Isis and the former king, Osiris. By law, the throne is rightfully mine.
My son is right. He should receive his father's inheritance!
Horus is too young and inexperienced to be our leader. I alone have shown the power and courage of a true king.
The gods argued for hours to determine the rightful king. But they could not reach an agreement.
Let's settle this. Horus, I challenge you to a series of contests. The winner will be king.
I accept your offer, Seth. May the better man win.
So be it.

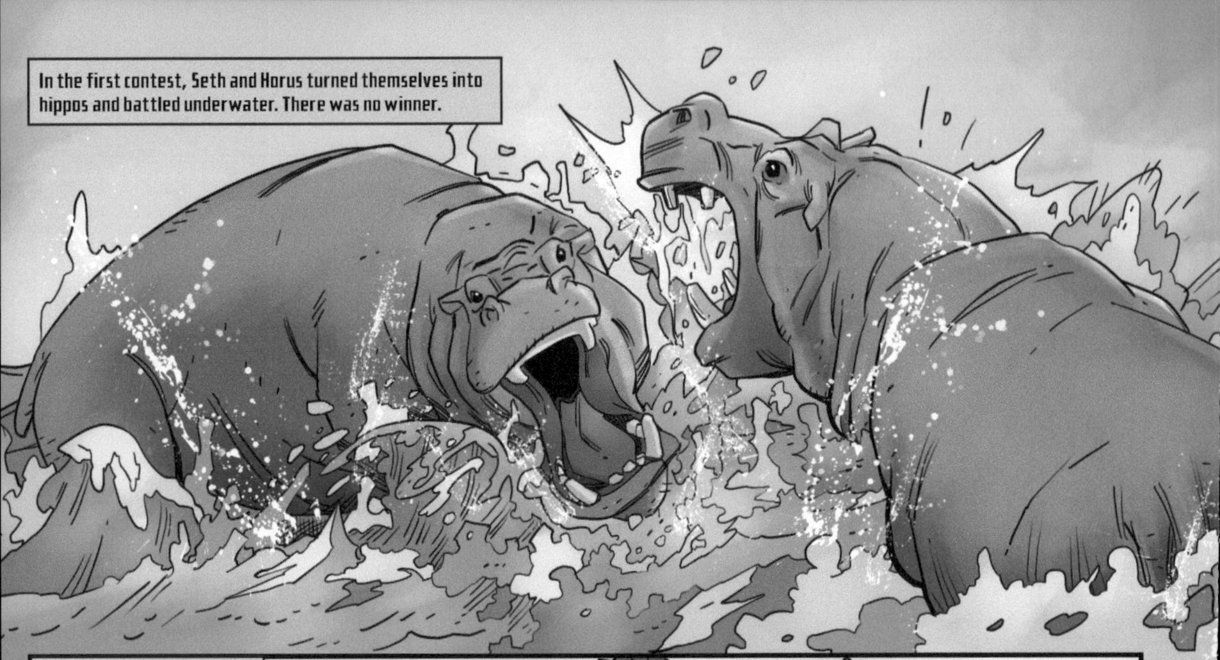
In the first contest, Seth and Horus turned themselves into hippos and battled underwater. There was no winner.

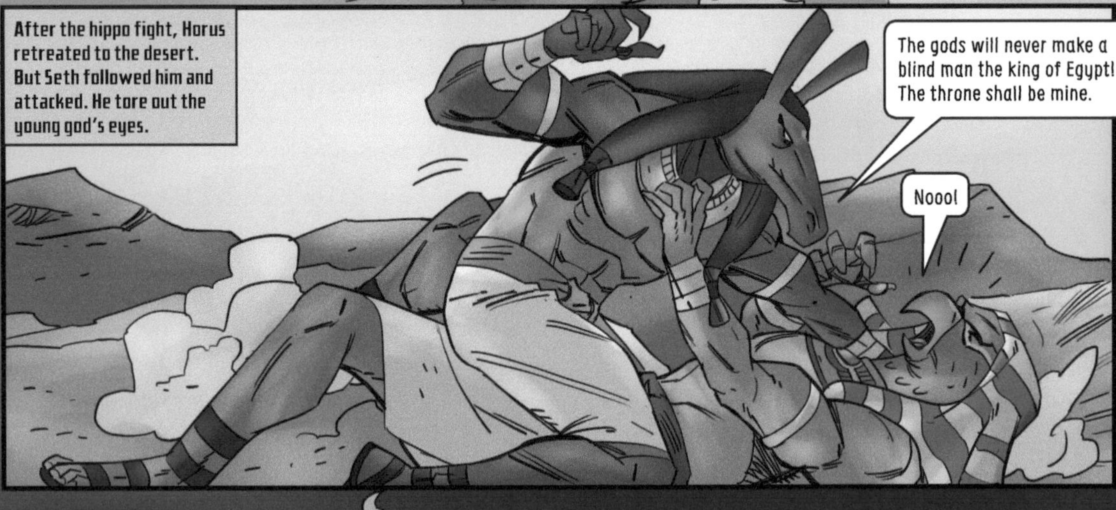
After the hippo fight, Horus retreated to the desert. But Seth followed him and attacked. He tore out the young god's eyes.
The gods will never make a blind man the king of Egypt! The throne shall be mine.
Nooo!

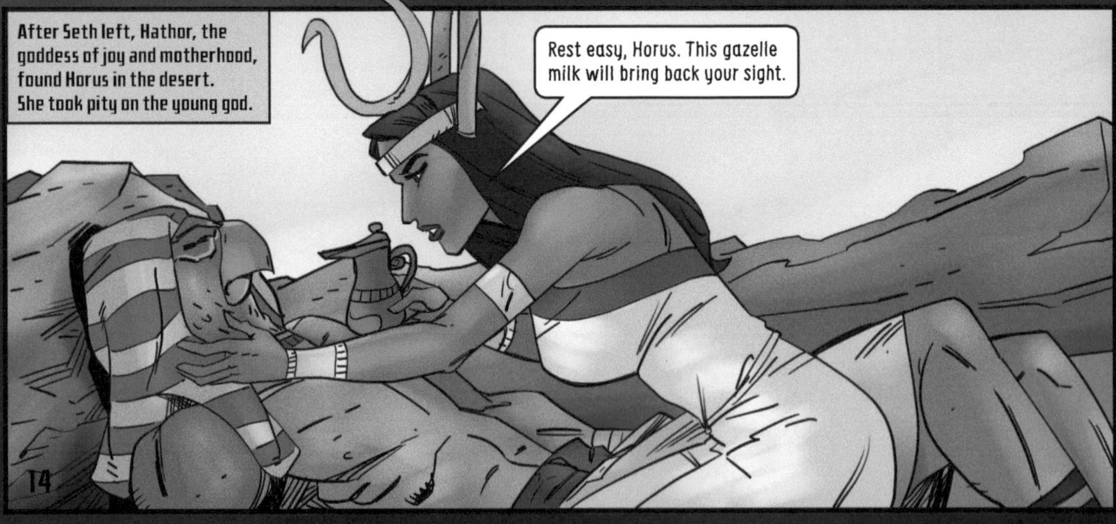
After Seth left, Hathor, the goddess of joy and motherhood, found Horus in the desert. She took pity on the young god.
Rest easy, Horus. This gazelle milk will bring back your sight.

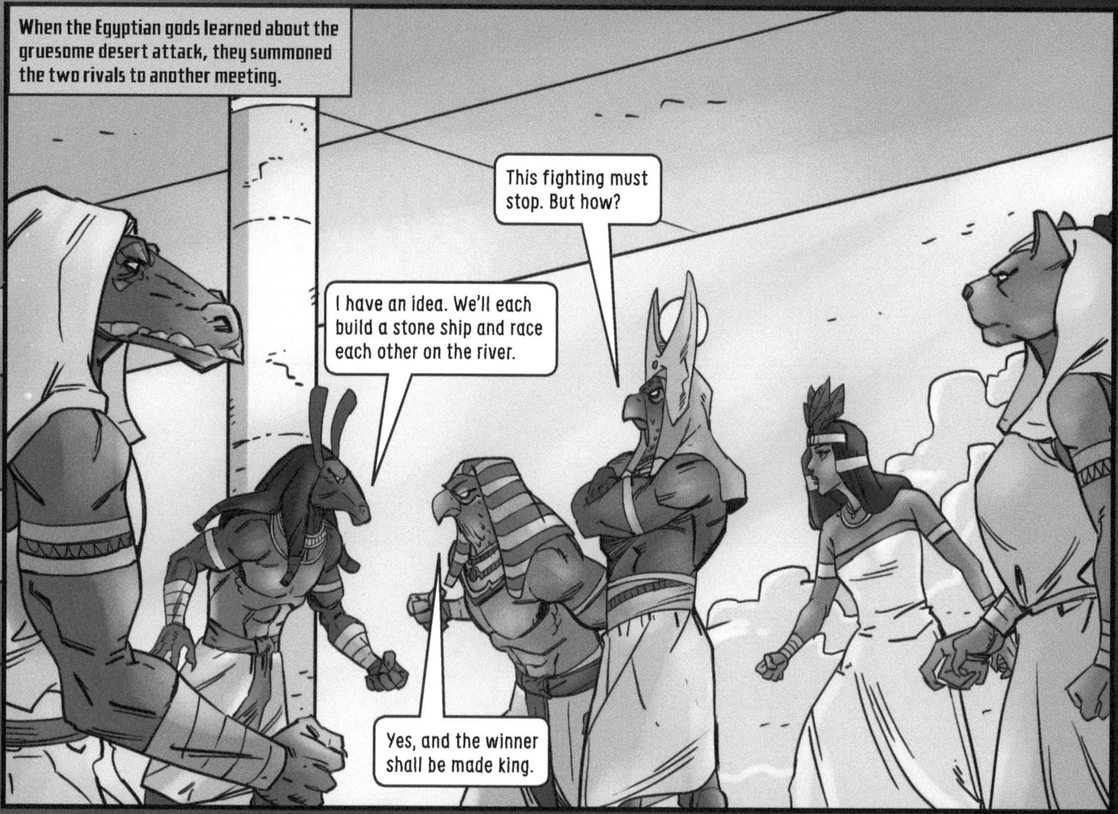
When the Egyptian gods learned about the gruesome desert attack, they summoned the two rivals to another meeting.
This fighting must stop. But how?
I have an idea. We'll each build a stone ship and race each other on the river.
Yes, and the winner shall be made king.

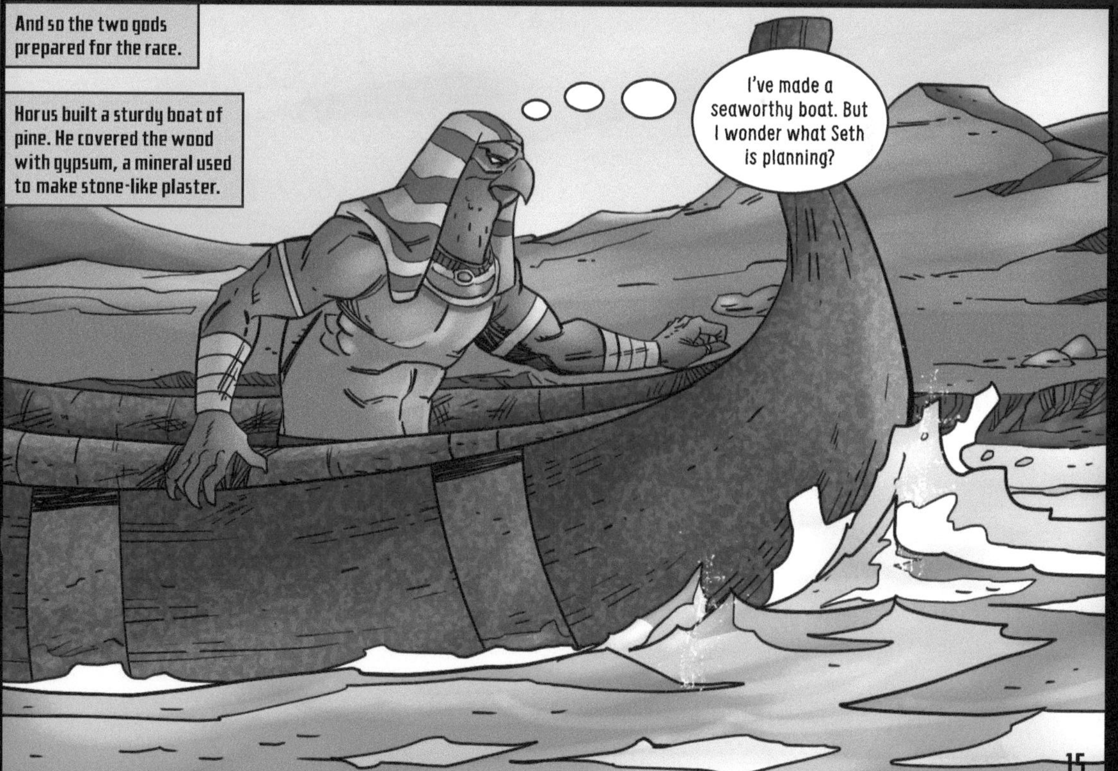
And so the two gods prepared for the race.
Horus built a sturdy boat of pine. He covered the wood with gypsum, a mineral used to make stone-like plaster.
I've made a seaworthy boat. But I wonder what Seth is planning?

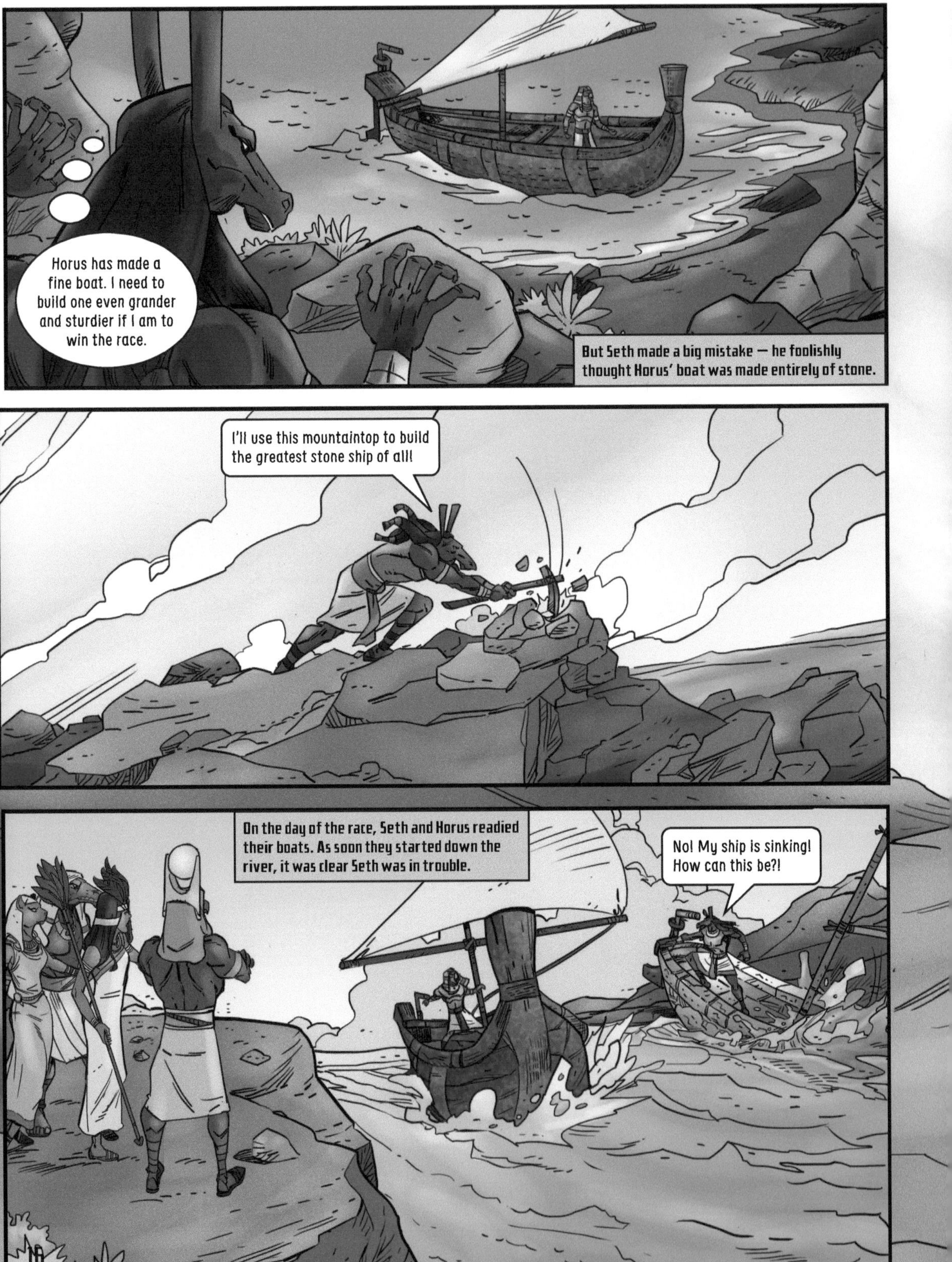
Horus has made a fine boat. I need to build one even grander and sturdier if I am to win the race.
But Seth made a big mistake — he foolishly thought Horus' boat was made entirely of stone.
I'll use this mountaintop to build the greatest stone ship of all!
On the day of the race, Seth and Horus readied their boats. As soon they started down the river, it was clear Seth was in trouble.
No! My ship is sinking! How can this be?!

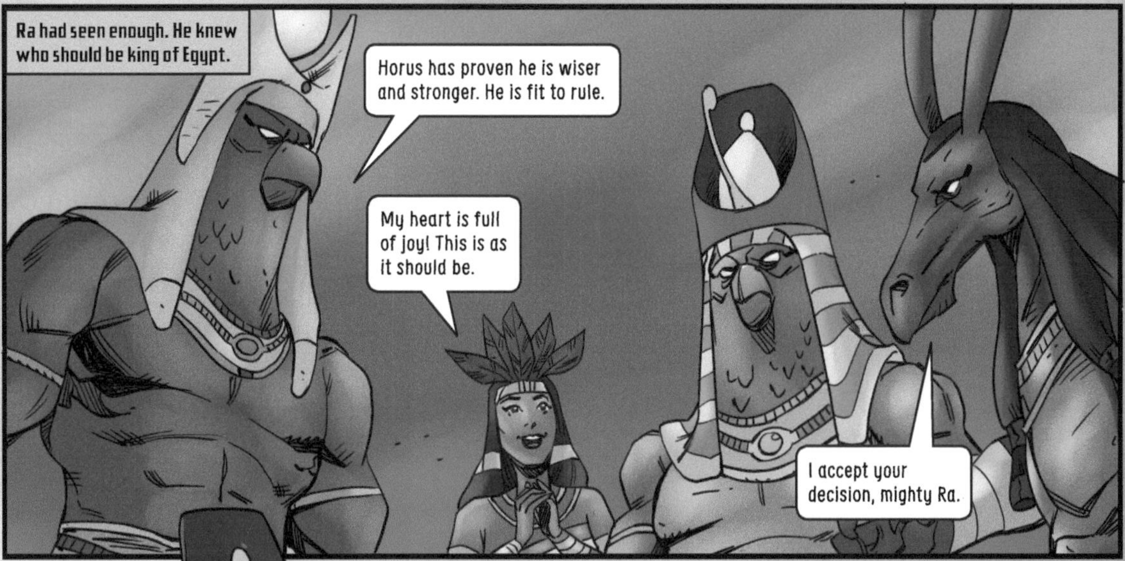
Ra had seen enough. He knew who should be king of Egypt.
Horus has proven he is wiser and stronger. He is fit to rule.
My heart is full of joy! This is as it should be.
I accept your decision, mighty Ra.

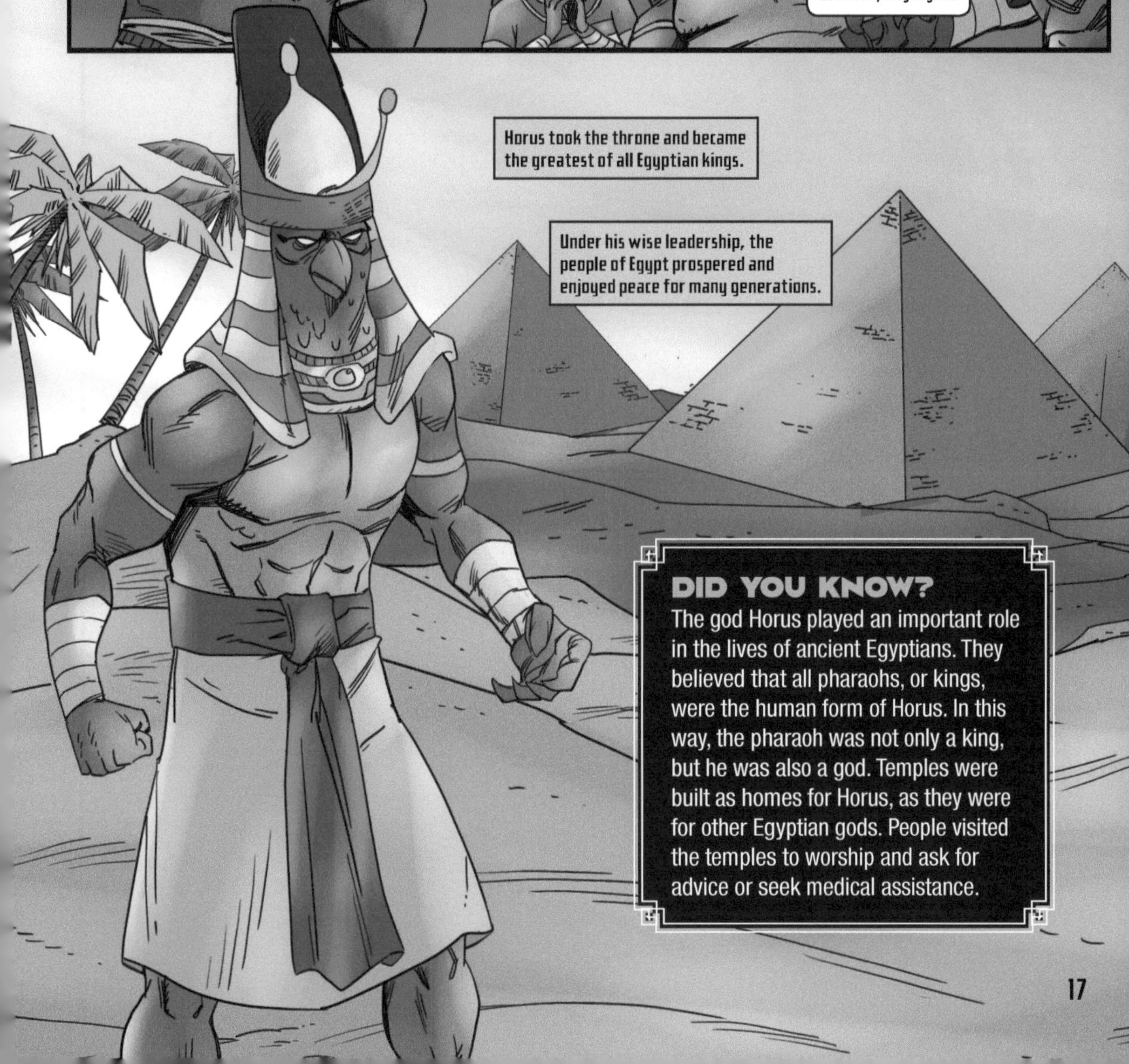
Horus took the throne and became the greatest of all Egyptian kings.
Under his wise leadership, the people of Egypt prospered and enjoyed peace for many generations.

DID YOU KNOW?

The god Horus played an important role in the lives of ancient Egyptians. They believed that all pharaohs, or kings, were the human form of Horus. In this way, the pharaoh was not only a king, but he was also a god. Temples were built as homes for Horus, as they were for other Egyptian gods. People visited the temples to worship and ask for advice or seek medical assistance.

CHAPTER THREE

THE BATTLE OF VELES AND PERUN

A SLAVIC MYTH

SLAVIC PEOPLES LIVE IN CENTRAL EUROPE AND EASTWARD INTO CENTRAL ASIA, INCLUDING RUSSIA. IN THE FOLLOWING MYTH TOLD BY THE SLAVS, TWO GODS WERE LOCKED IN A NEVER-ENDING BATTLE. THE ONGOING FEUD BETWEEN THE MIGHTY GODS PERUN AND VELES REPRESENTED THE ETERNAL STRUGGLE BETWEEN ORDER AND CHAOS.

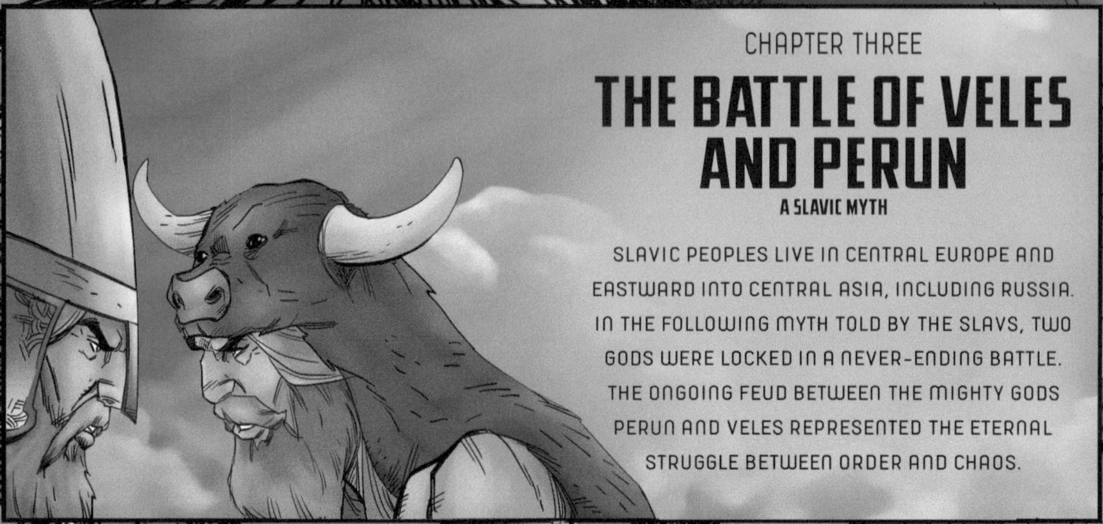

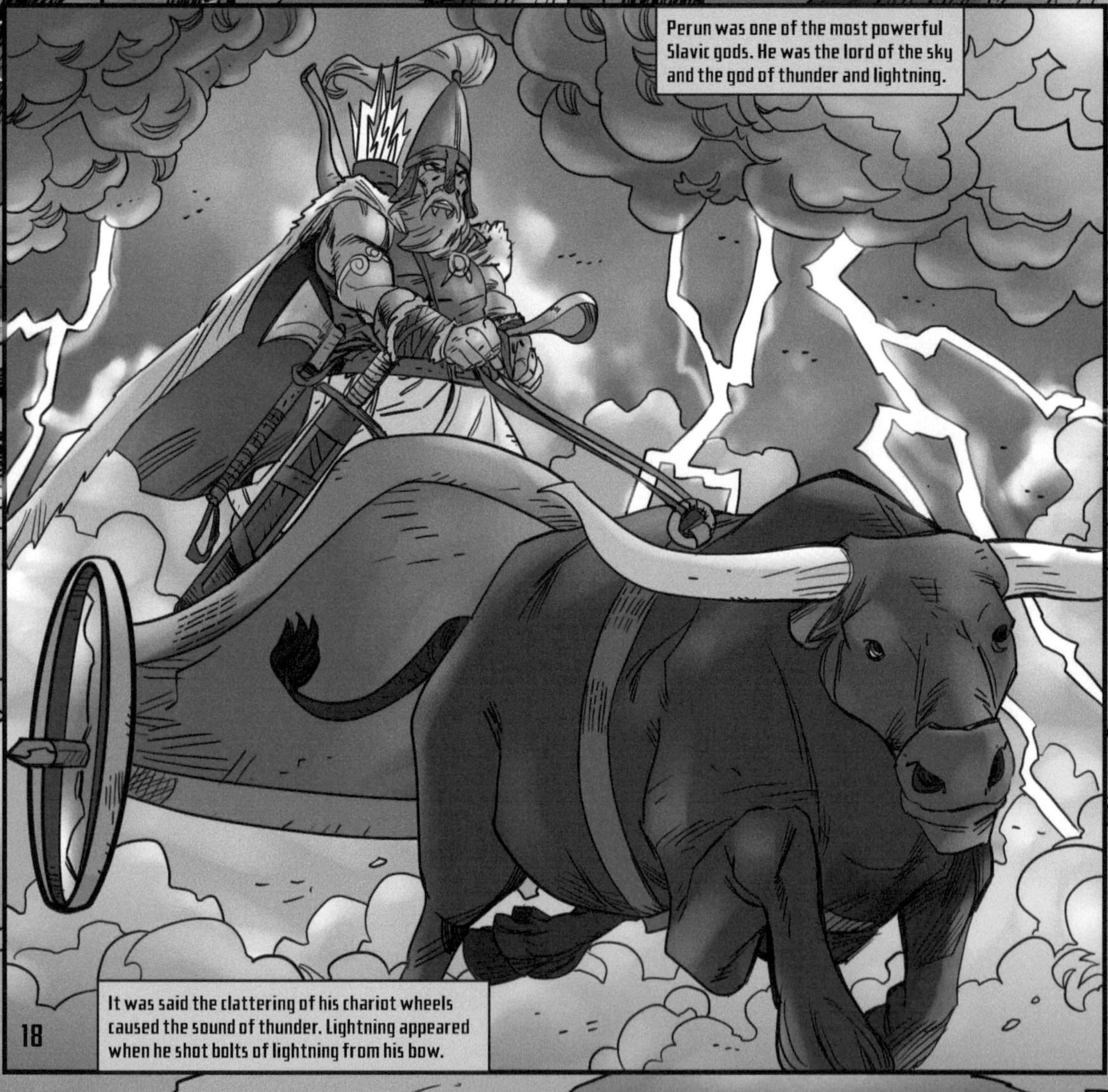
Perun was one of the most powerful Slavic gods. He was the lord of the sky and the god of thunder and lightning.
It was said the clattering of his chariot wheels caused the sound of thunder. Lightning appeared when he shot bolts of lightning from his bow.

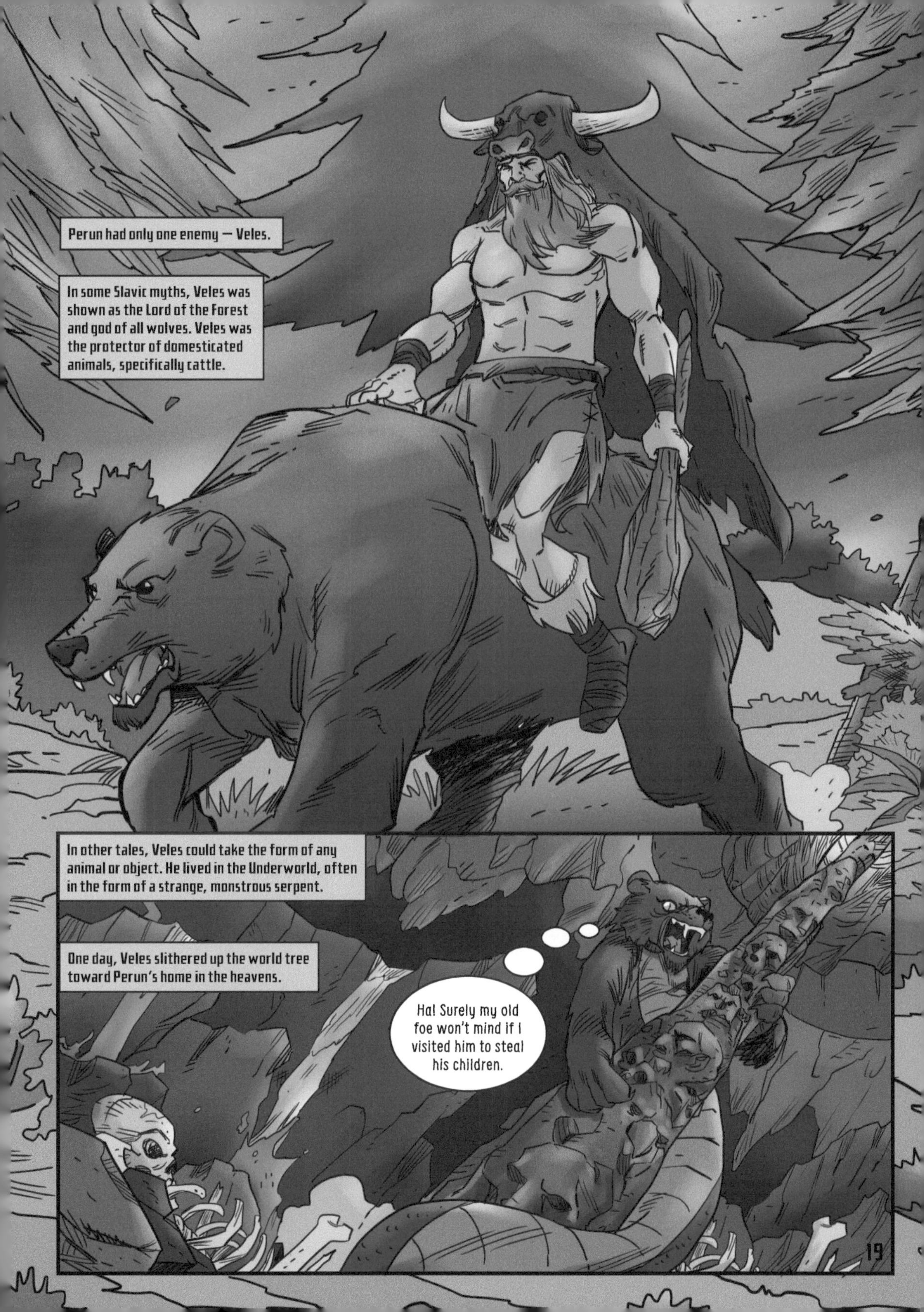
Perun had only one enemy — Veles.
In some Slavic myths, Veles was shown as the Lord of the Forest and god of all wolves. Veles was the protector of domesticated animals, specifically cattle.
In other tales, Veles could take the form of any animal or object. He lived in the Underworld, often in the form of a strange, monstrous serpent.
One day, Veles slithered up the world tree toward Perun's home in the heavens.
Ha! Surely my old foe won't mind if I visited him to steal his children.

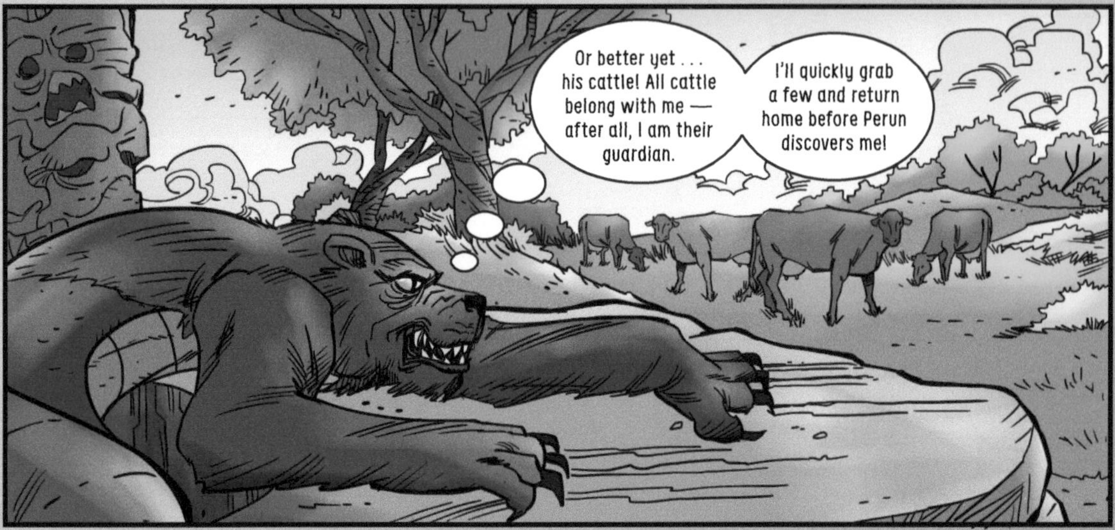
Or better yet . . . his cattle! All cattle belong with me — after all, I am their guardian.
I'll quickly grab a few and return home before Perun discovers me!

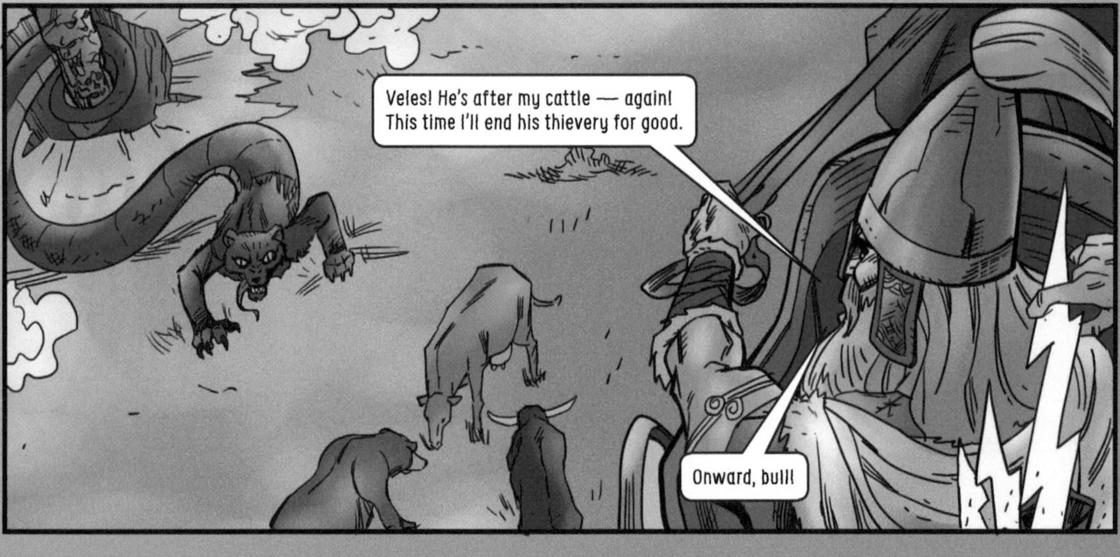
Veles! He's after my cattle — again! This time I'll end his thievery for good.
Onward, bull!

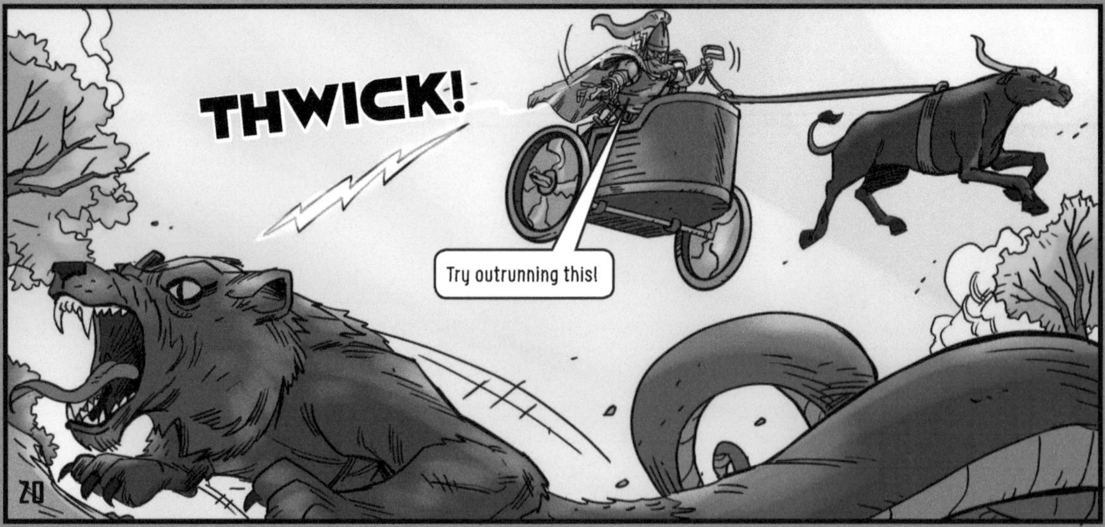
THWICK!
Try outrunning this!

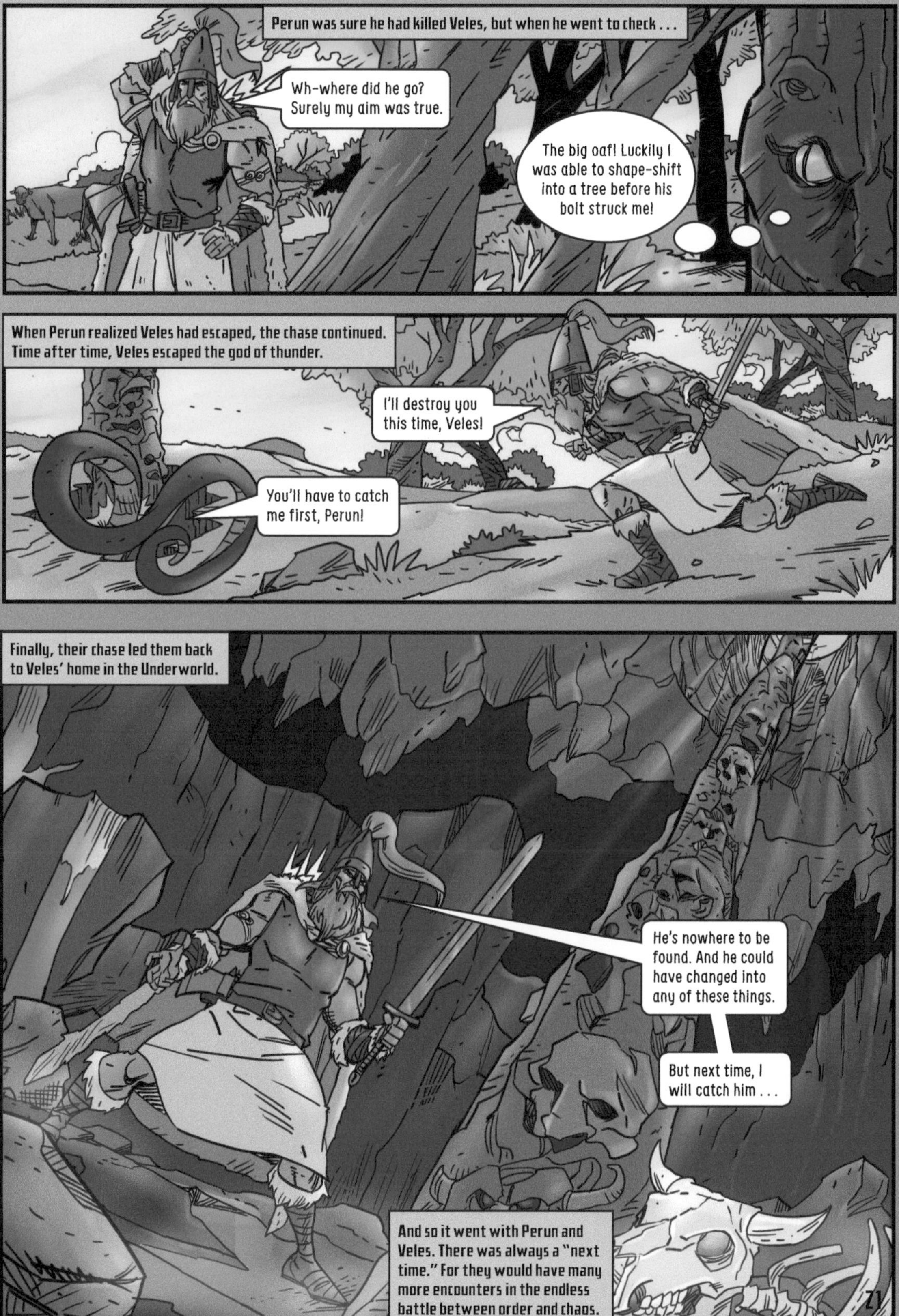
Perun was sure he had killed Veles, but when he went to check . . .
Wh-where did he go? Surely my aim was true.
The big oaf! Luckily I was able to shape-shift into a tree before his bolt struck me!
When Perun realized Veles had escaped, the chase continued. Time after time, Veles escaped the god of thunder.
I'll destroy you this time, Veles!
You'll have to catch me first, Perun!
Finally, their chase led them back to Veles' home in the Underworld.
He's nowhere to be found. And he could have changed into any of these things.
But next time, I will catch him . . .
And so it went with Perun and Veles. There was always a "next time." For they would have many more encounters in the endless battle between order and chaos.

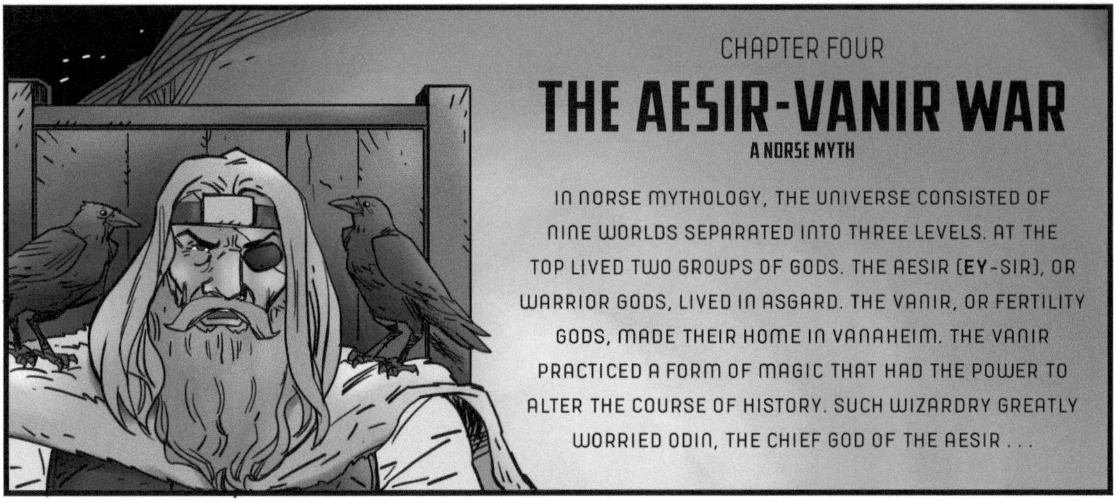
CHAPTER FOUR
THE AESIR-VANIR WAR
A NORSE MYTH
IN NORSE MYTHOLOGY, THE UNIVERSE CONSISTED OF NINE WORLDS SEPARATED INTO THREE LEVELS. AT THE TOP LIVED TWO GROUPS OF GODS. THE AESIR (EY-SIR), OR WARRIOR GODS, LIVED IN ASGARD. THE VANIR, OR FERTILITY GODS, MADE THEIR HOME IN VANAHEIM. THE VANIR PRACTICED A FORM OF MAGIC THAT HAD THE POWER TO ALTER THE COURSE OF HISTORY. SUCH WIZARDRY GREATLY WORRIED ODIN, THE CHIEF GOD OF THE AESIR . . .

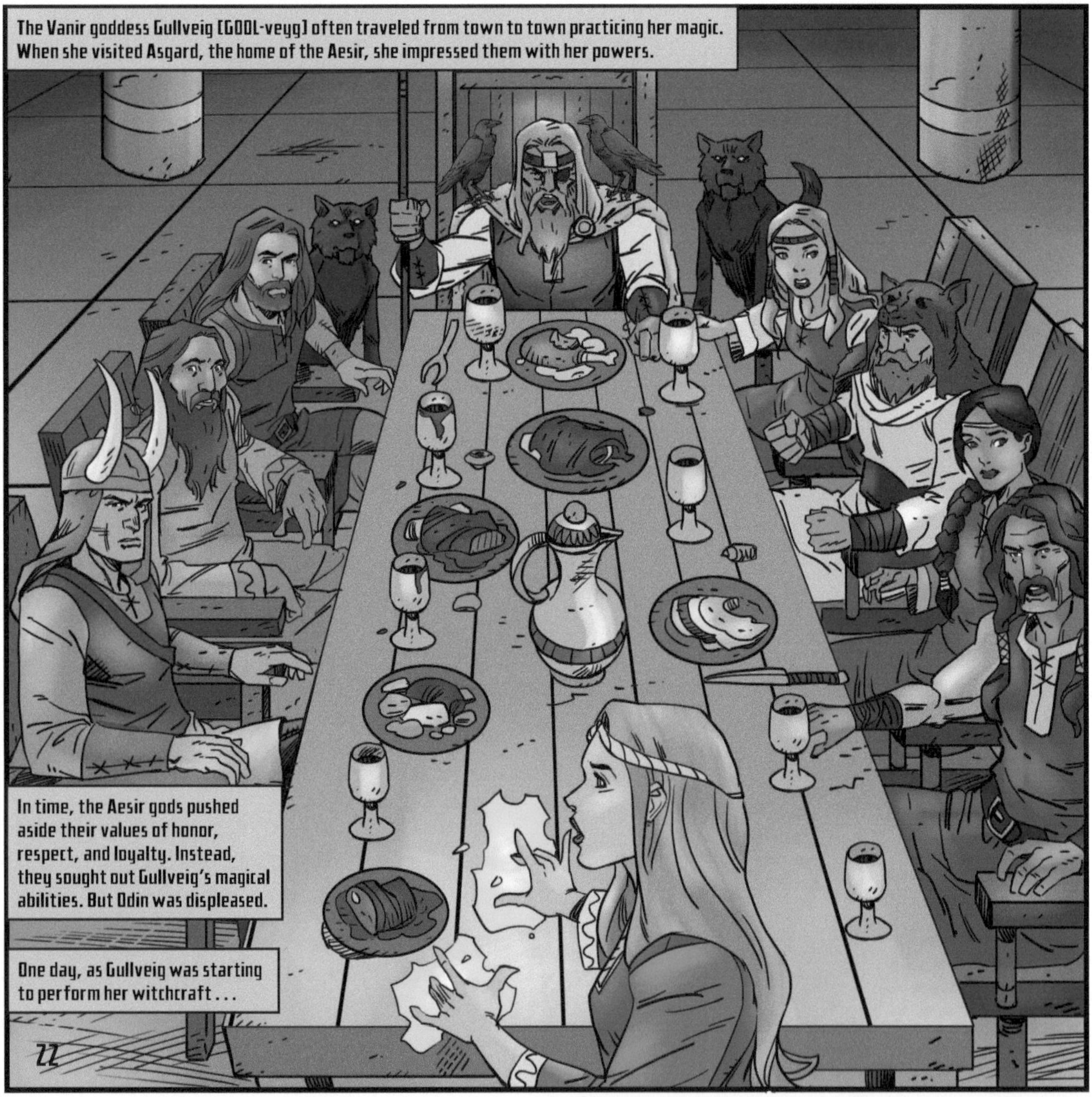
The Vanir goddess Gullveig (GOOL-veyg) often traveled from town to town practicing her magic. When she visited Asgard, the home of the Aesir, she impressed them with her powers.
In time, the Aesir gods pushed aside their values of honor, respect, and loyalty. Instead, they sought out Gullveig's magical abilities. But Odin was displeased.
One day, as Gullveig was starting to perform her witchcraft . . .

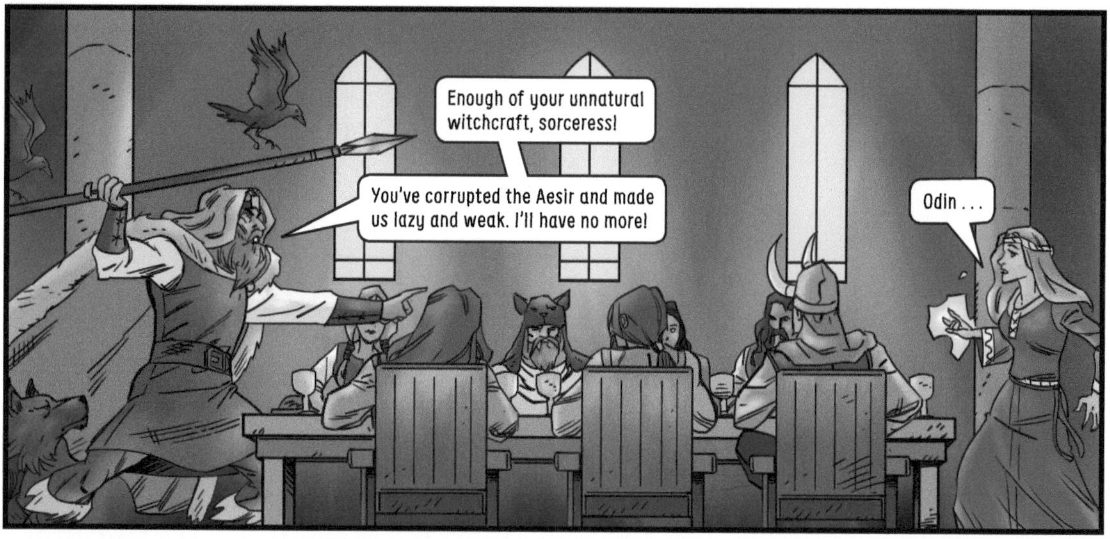
Enough of your unnatural witchcraft, sorceress!
You've corrupted the Aesir and made us lazy and weak. I'll have no more!
Odin . . .

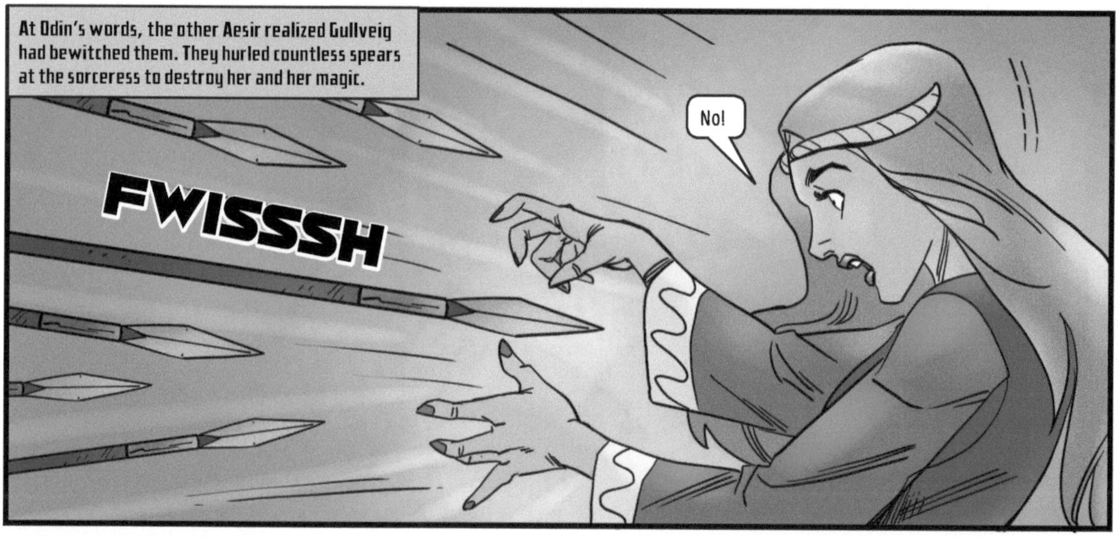
At Odin's words, the other Aesir realized Gullveig had bewitched them. They hurled countless spears at the sorceress to destroy her and her magic.
No!
FWISSSH

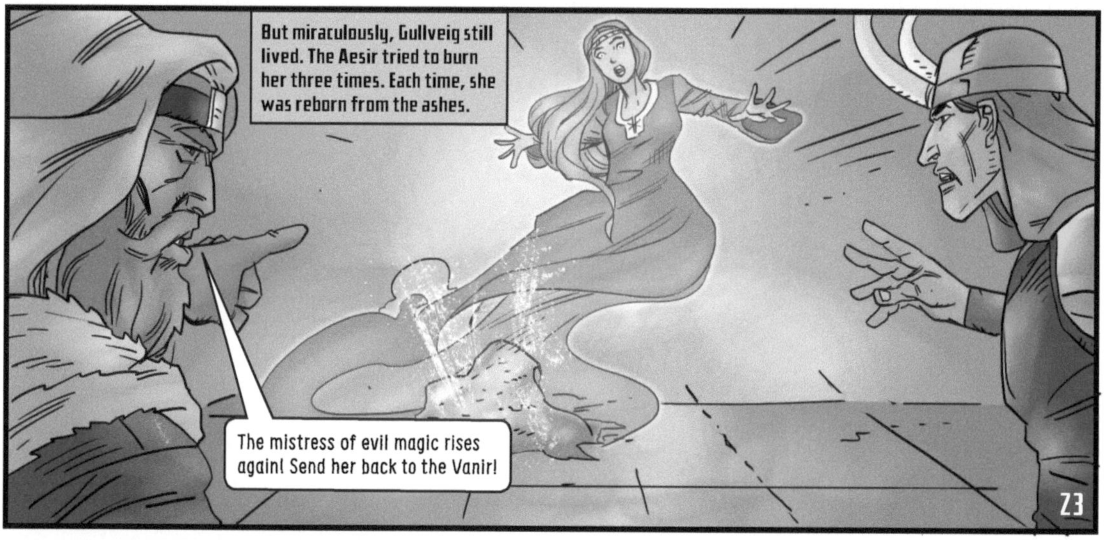
But miraculously, Gullveig still lived. The Aesir tried to burn her three times. Each time, she was reborn from the ashes.
The mistress of evil magic rises again! Send her back to the Vanir!

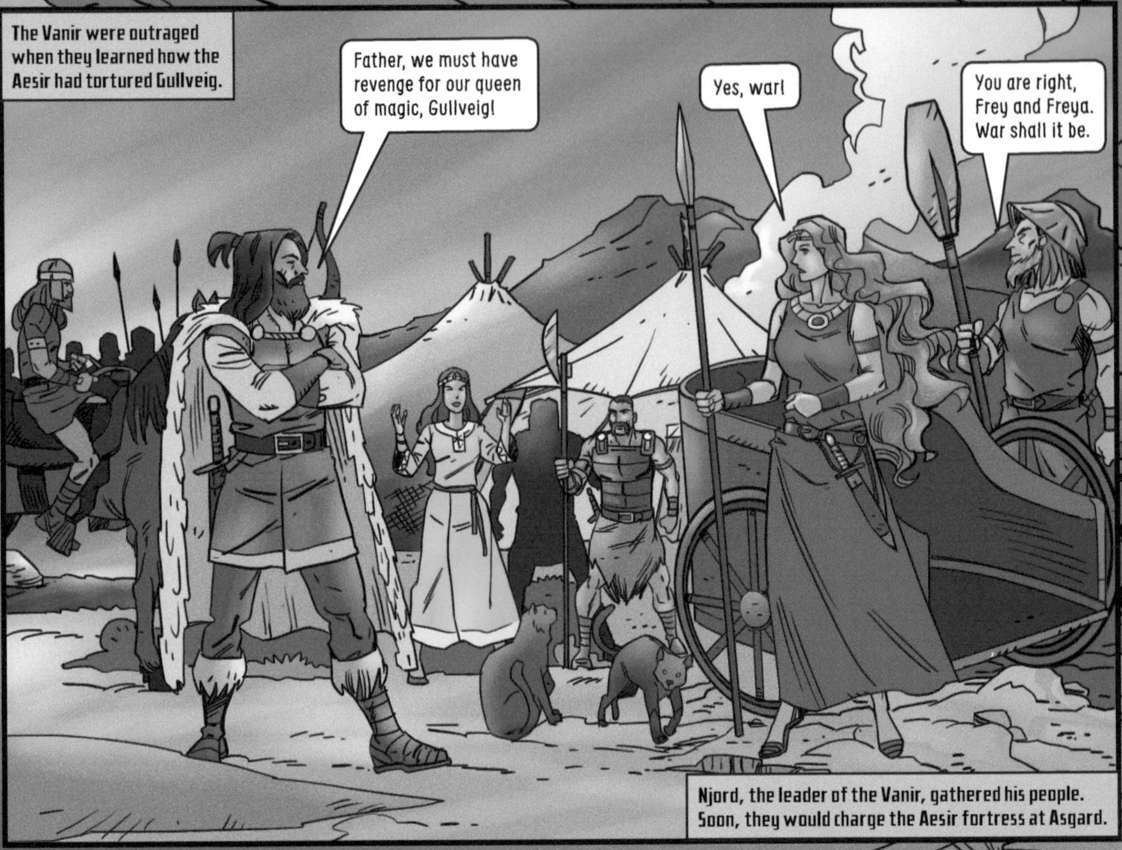
The Vanir were outraged when they learned how the Aesir had tortured Gullveig.
Father, we must have revenge for our queen of magic, Gullveig!
Yes, war!
You are right, Frey and Freya. War shall it be.
Njord, the leader of the Vanir, gathered his people. Soon, they would charge the Aesir fortress at Asgard.

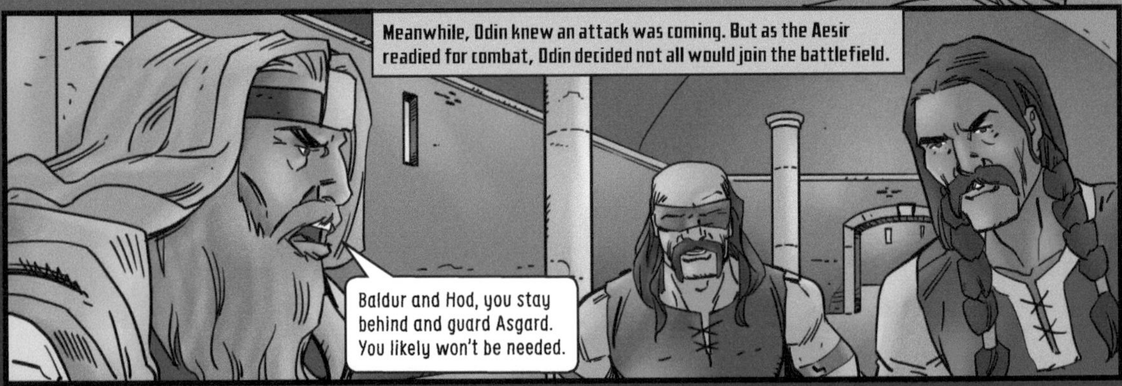
Meanwhile, Odin knew an attack was coming. But as the Aesir readied for combat, Odin decided not all would join the battlefield.
Baldur and Hod, you stay behind and guard Asgard. You likely won't be needed.

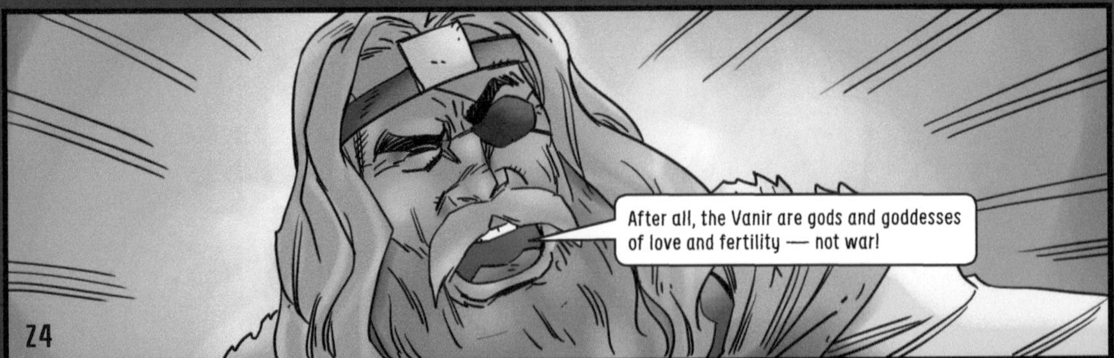
After all, the Vanir are gods and goddesses of love and fertility — not war!

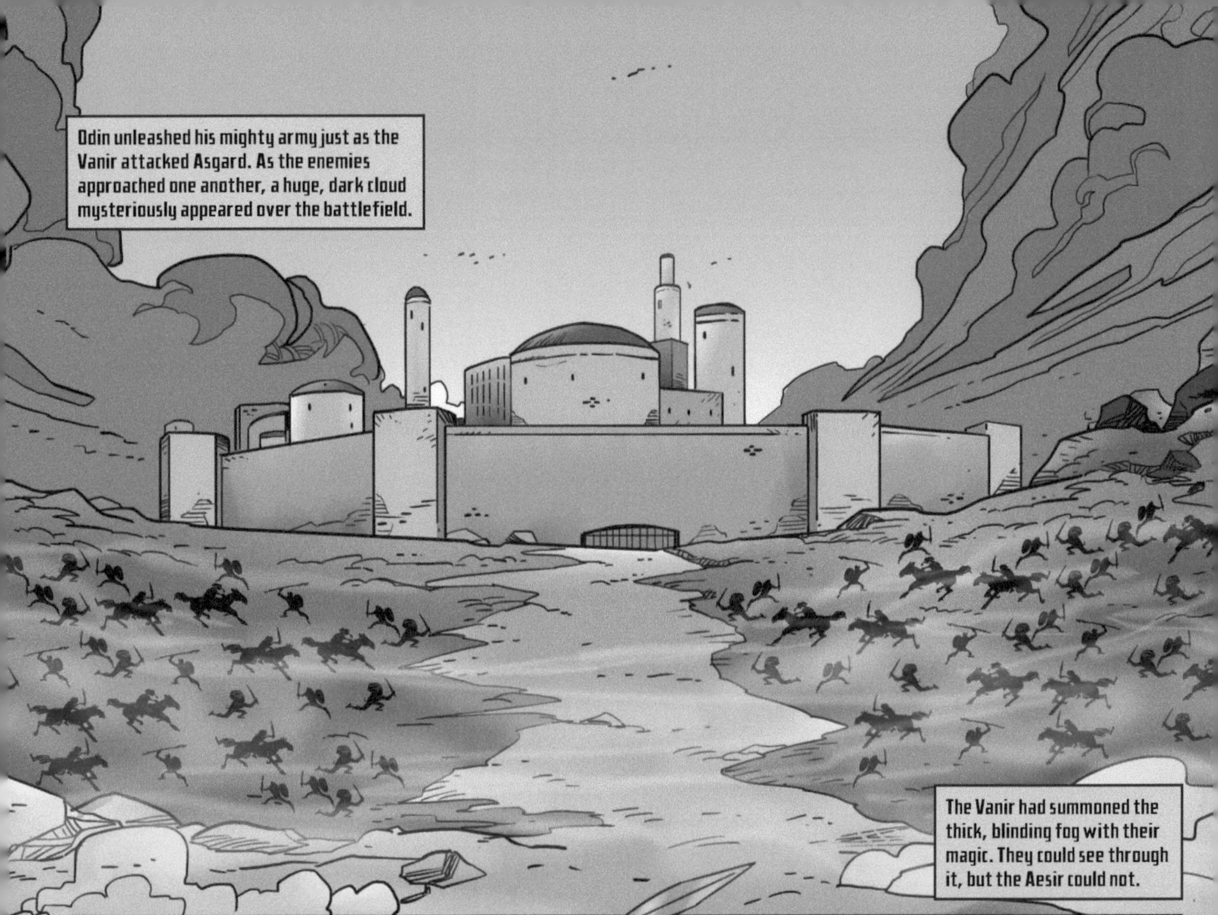
Odin unleashed his mighty army just as the Vanir attacked Asgard. As the enemies approached one another, a huge, dark cloud mysteriously appeared over the battlefield.
The Vanir had summoned the thick, blinding fog with their magic. They could see through it, but the Aesir could not.

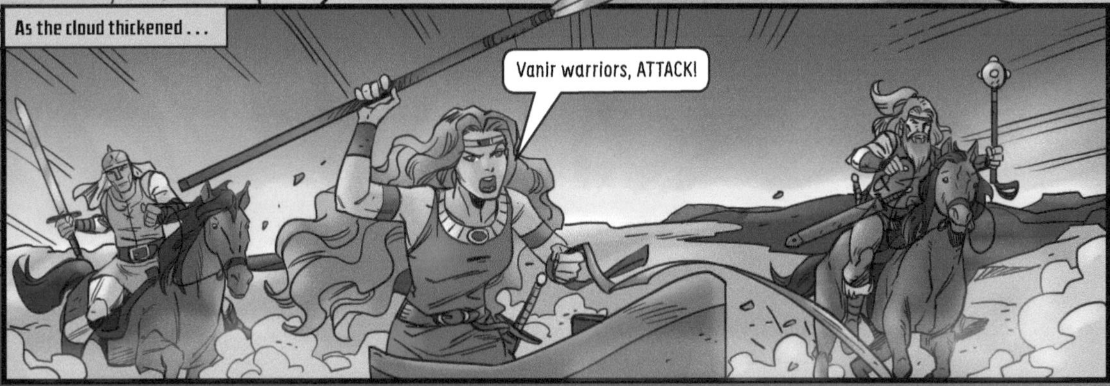
As the cloud thickened . . .
Vanir warriors, ATTACK!

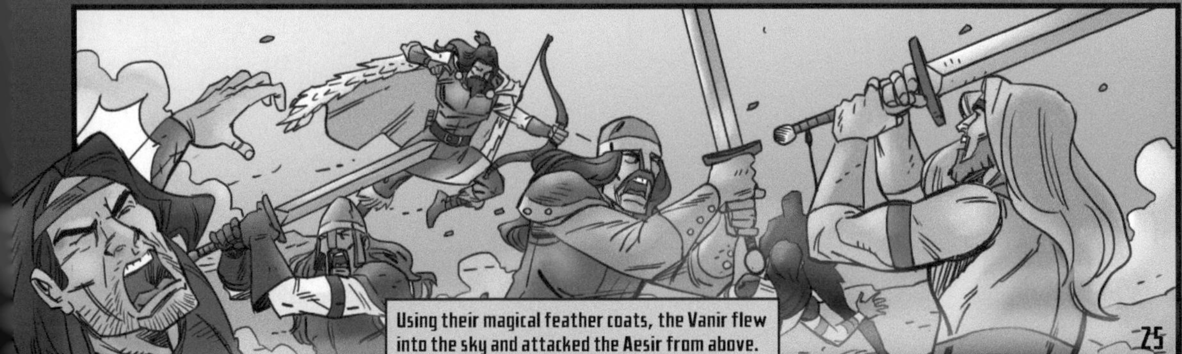
Using their magical feather coats, the Vanir flew into the sky and attacked the Aesir from above.

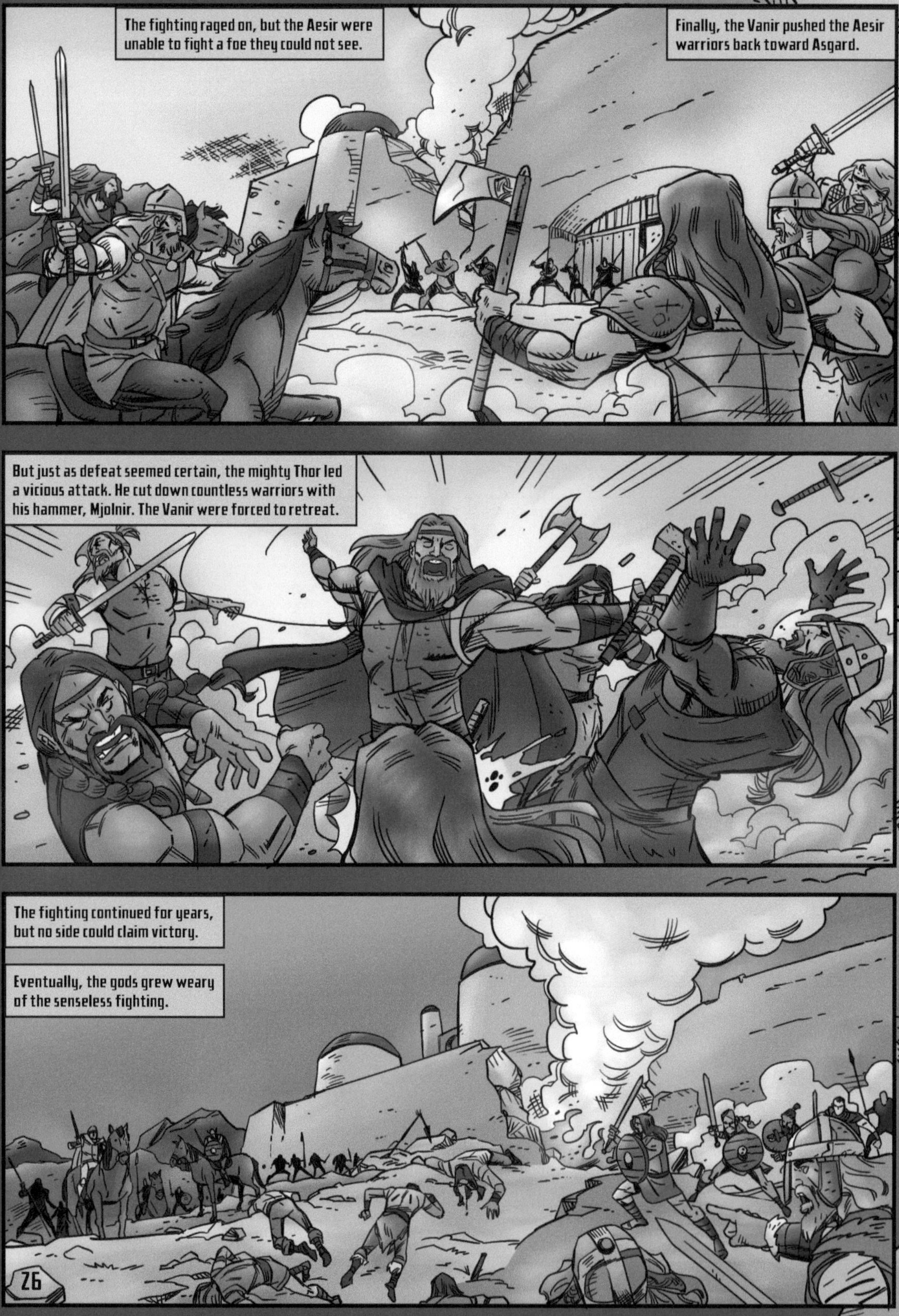
The fighting raged on, but the Aesir were unable to fight a foe they could not see.
Finally, the Vanir pushed the Aesir warriors back toward Asgard.
But just as defeat seemed certain, the mighty Thor led a vicious attack. He cut down countless warriors with his hammer, Mjolnir. The Vanir were forced to retreat.
The fighting continued for years, but no side could claim victory.
Eventually, the gods grew weary of the senseless fighting.

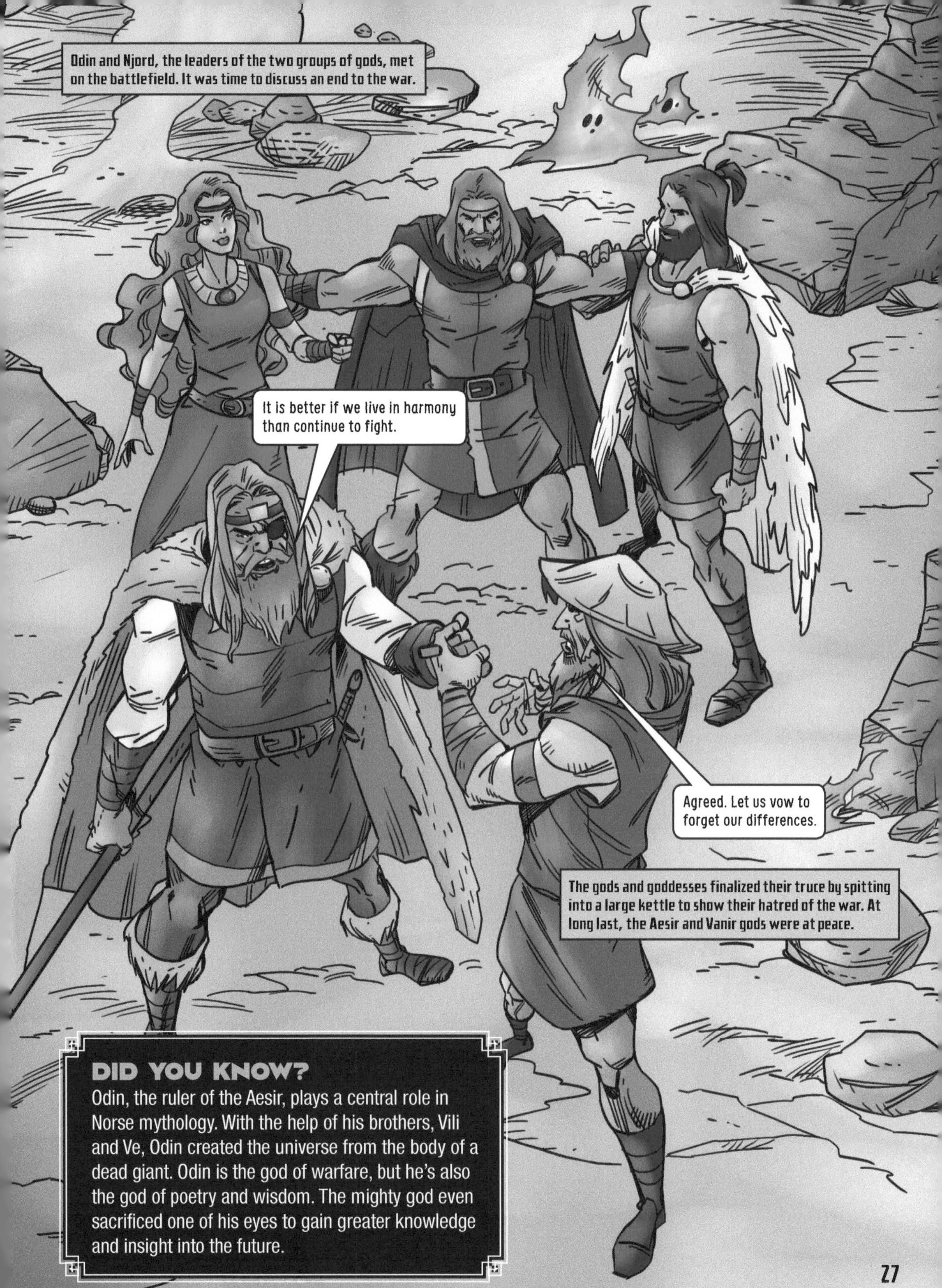
Odin and Njord, the leaders of the two groups of gods, met on the battlefield. It was time to discuss an end to the war.
It is better if we live in harmony than continue to fight.
Agreed. Let us vow to forget our differences.
The gods and goddesses finalized their truce by spitting into a large kettle to show their hatred of the war. At long last, the Aesir and Vanir gods were at peace.

DID YOU KNOW?

Odin, the ruler of the Aesir, plays a central role in Norse mythology. With the help of his brothers, Vili and Ve, Odin created the universe from the body of a dead giant. Odin is the god of warfare, but he's also the god of poetry and wisdom. The mighty god even sacrificed one of his eyes to gain greater knowledge and insight into the future.

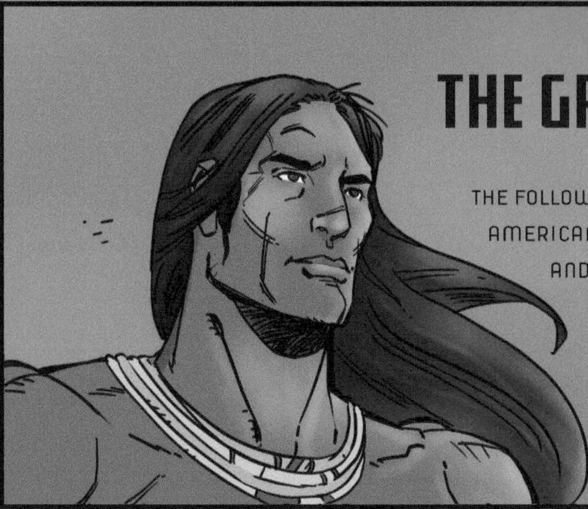

CHAPTER FIVE

THE GREAT MYSTERY POWER

A TOHONO O'ODHAM MYTH

THE FOLLOWING STORY IS BASED ON A MYTH FROM THE NATIVE AMERICAN TOHONO O'ODHAM PEOPLES OF SOUTHERN ARIZONA AND NORTHWESTERN MEXICO. IN THIS TALE, THE GREAT MONTEZUMA (MON-TEE-**SOO**-MAH) ANGERED THE SUPREME GOD AND CREATOR OF ALL, THE GREAT MYSTERY POWER. AFTER BEING PATIENT WITH THE OTHER GOD, THE GREAT MYSTERY POWER WAS FORCED TO TAKE EXTREME ACTIONS.

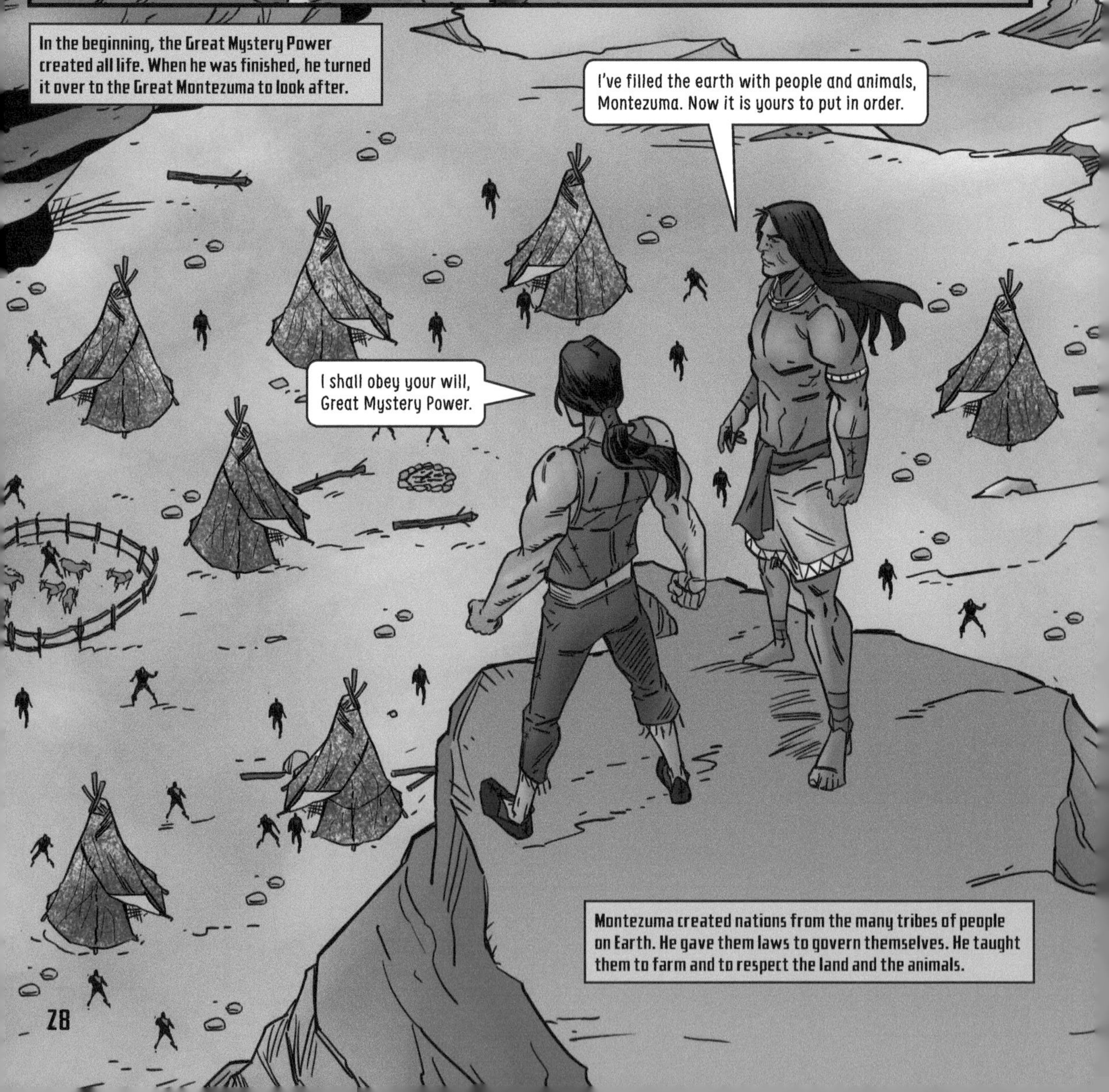
In the beginning, the Great Mystery Power created all life. When he was finished, he turned it over to the Great Montezuma to look after.
I've filled the earth with people and animals, Montezuma. Now it is yours to put in order.
I shall obey your will, Great Mystery Power.
Montezuma created nations from the many tribes of people on Earth. He gave them laws to govern themselves. He taught them to farm and to respect the land and the animals.

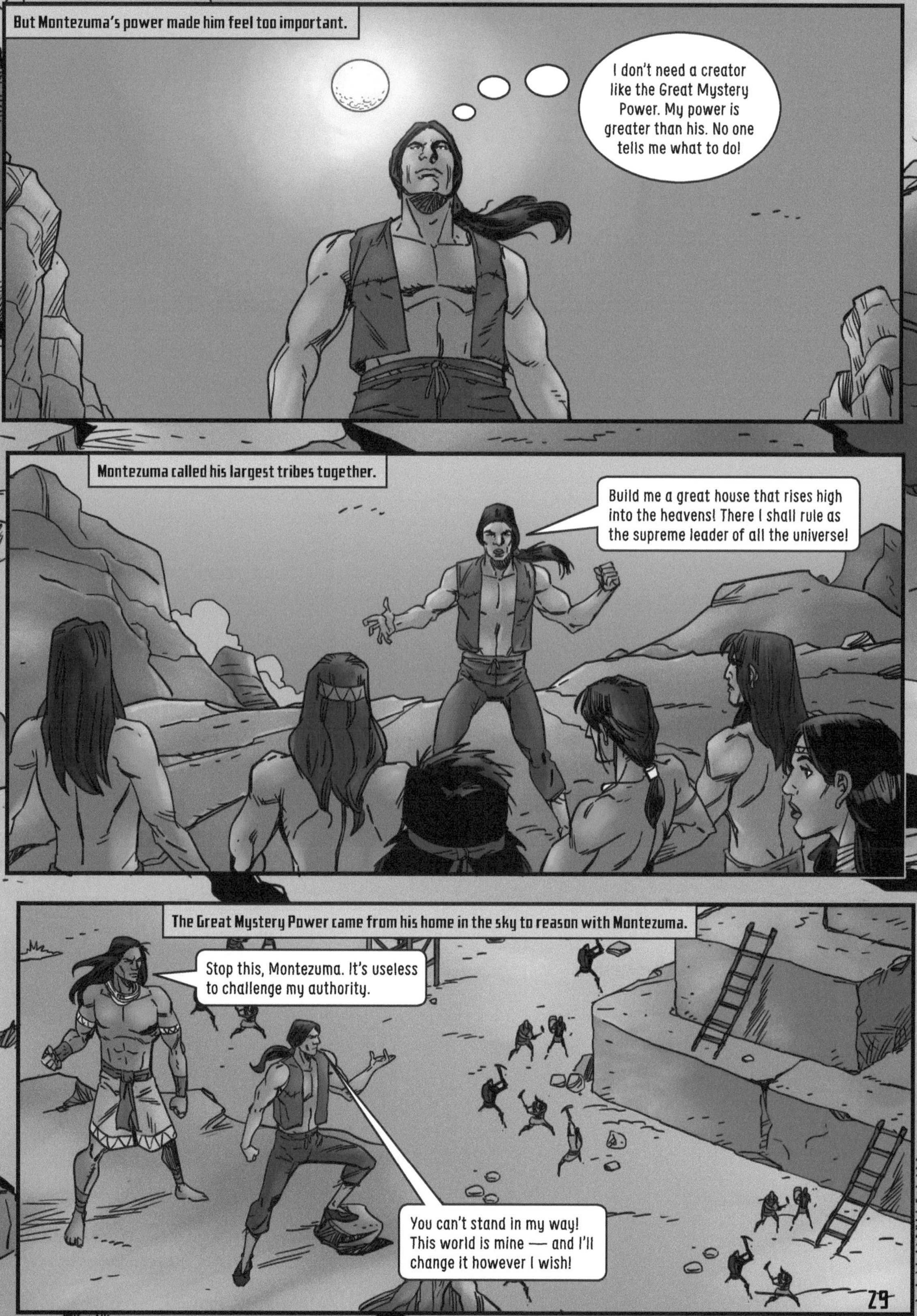

But Montezuma's power made him feel too important.
I don't need a creator like the Great Mystery Power. My power is greater than his. No one tells me what to do!
Montezuma called his largest tribes together.
Build me a great house that rises high into the heavens! There I shall rule as the supreme leader of all the universe!
The Great Mystery Power came from his home in the sky to reason with Montezuma.
Stop this, Montezuma. It's useless to challenge my authority.
You can't stand in my way! This world is mine — and I'll change it however I wish!

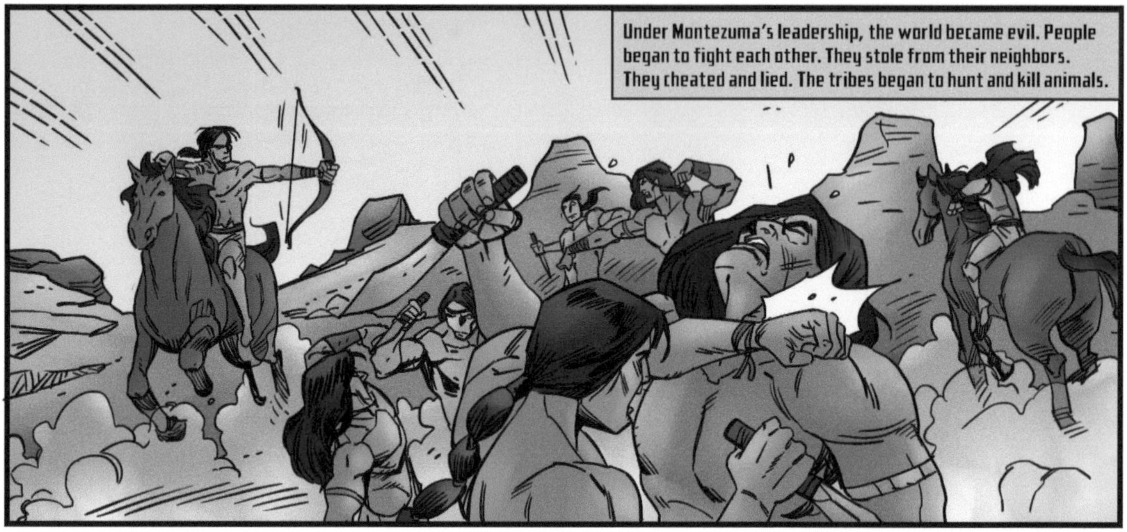
Under Montezuma's leadership, the world became evil. People began to fight each other. They stole from their neighbors. They cheated and lied. The tribes began to hunt and kill animals.

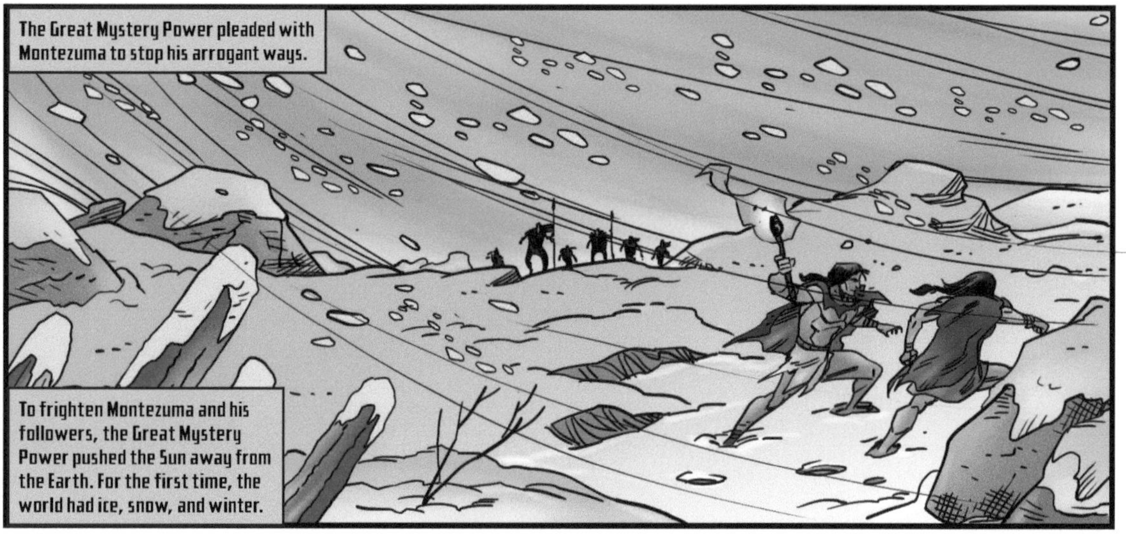
The Great Mystery Power pleaded with Montezuma to stop his arrogant ways.
To frighten Montezuma and his followers, the Great Mystery Power pushed the Sun away from the Earth. For the first time, the world had ice, snow, and winter.

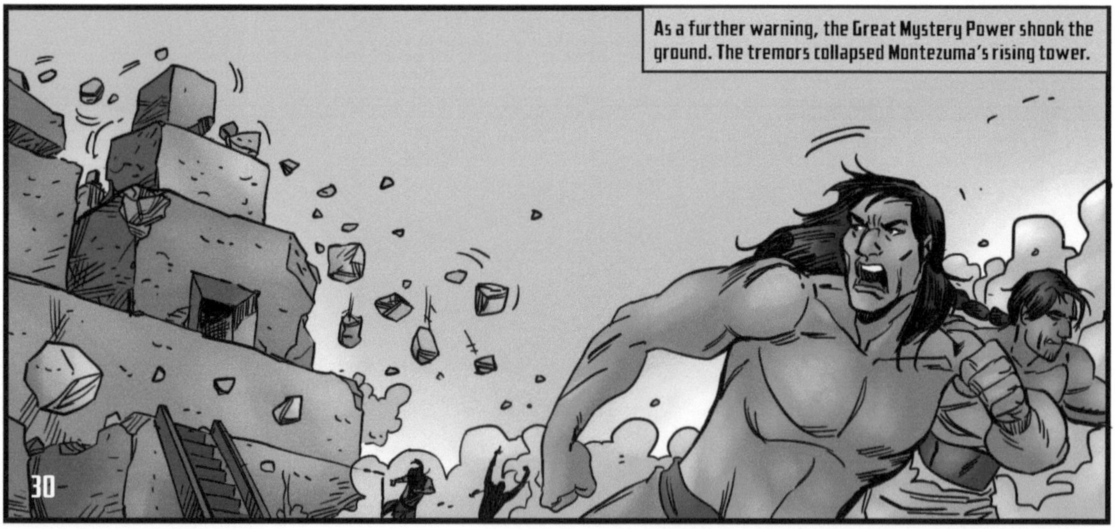
As a further warning, the Great Mystery Power shook the ground. The tremors collapsed Montezuma's rising tower.

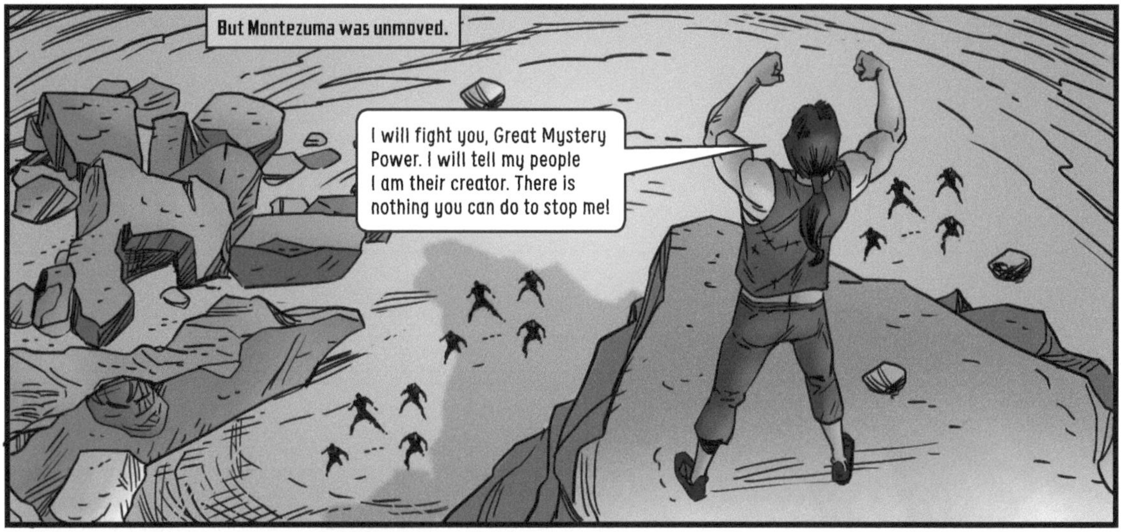
But Montezuma was unmoved.
I will fight you, Great Mystery Power. I will tell my people I am their creator. There is nothing you can do to stop me!

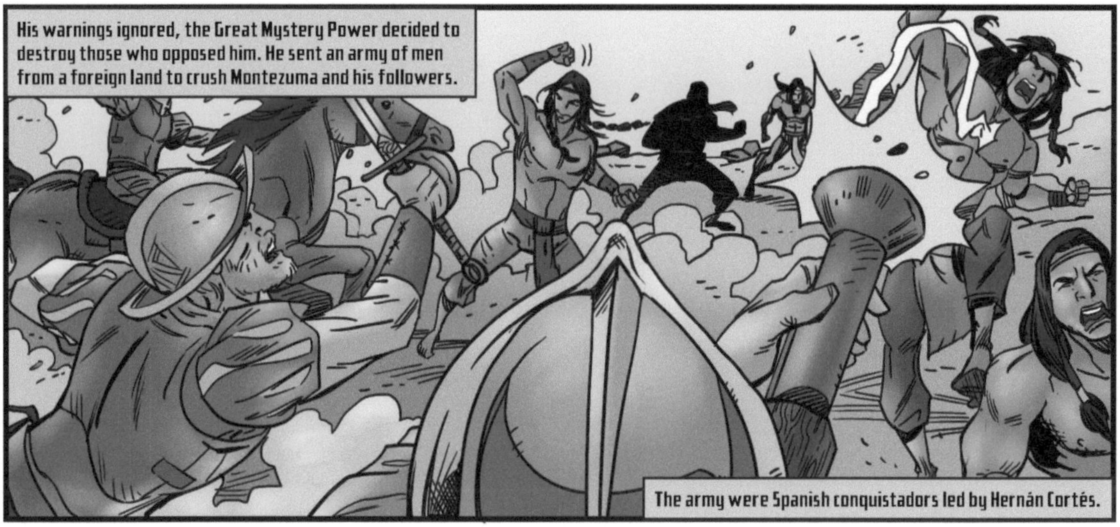
His warnings ignored, the Great Mystery Power decided to destroy those who opposed him. He sent an army of men from a foreign land to crush Montezuma and his followers.
The army were Spanish conquistadors led by Hernán Cortés.

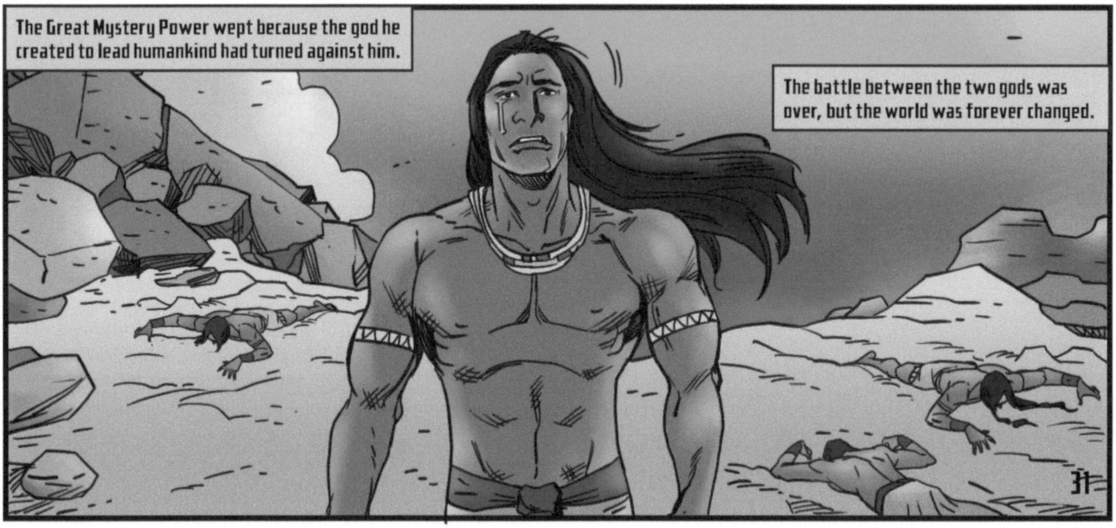
The Great Mystery Power wept because the god he created to lead humankind had turned against him.
The battle between the two gods was over, but the world was forever changed.

CHAPTER SIX

MARDUK FIGHTS THE GODDESS TIAMAT

A BABYLONIAN MYTH

THIS ANCIENT BABYLONIAN CREATION SAGA FROM THE *ENUMA ELISH* TELLS TWO STORIES. IT DESCRIBES HOW MARDUK BATTLED TO BECOME LEADER OF THE GODS, AND HOW HE WENT ON TO CREATE THE WORLD. THANKS TO HIS GREAT ACTS, MARDUK BECAME KNOWN AS THE CHIEF GOD OF BABYLON, THE COMMERCIAL AND POLITICAL CENTER OF THE POWERFUL BABYLONIAN EMPIRE.

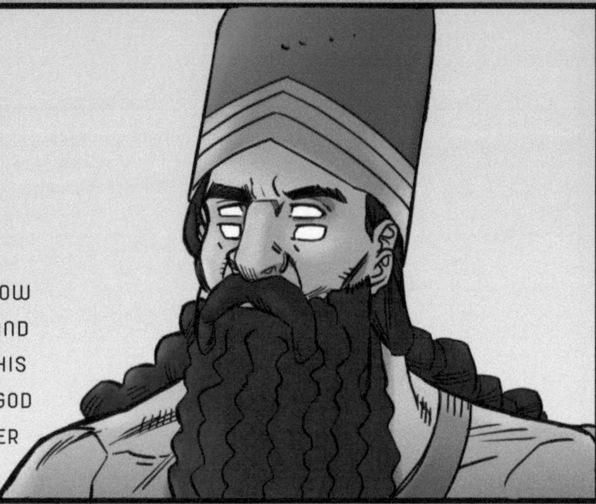

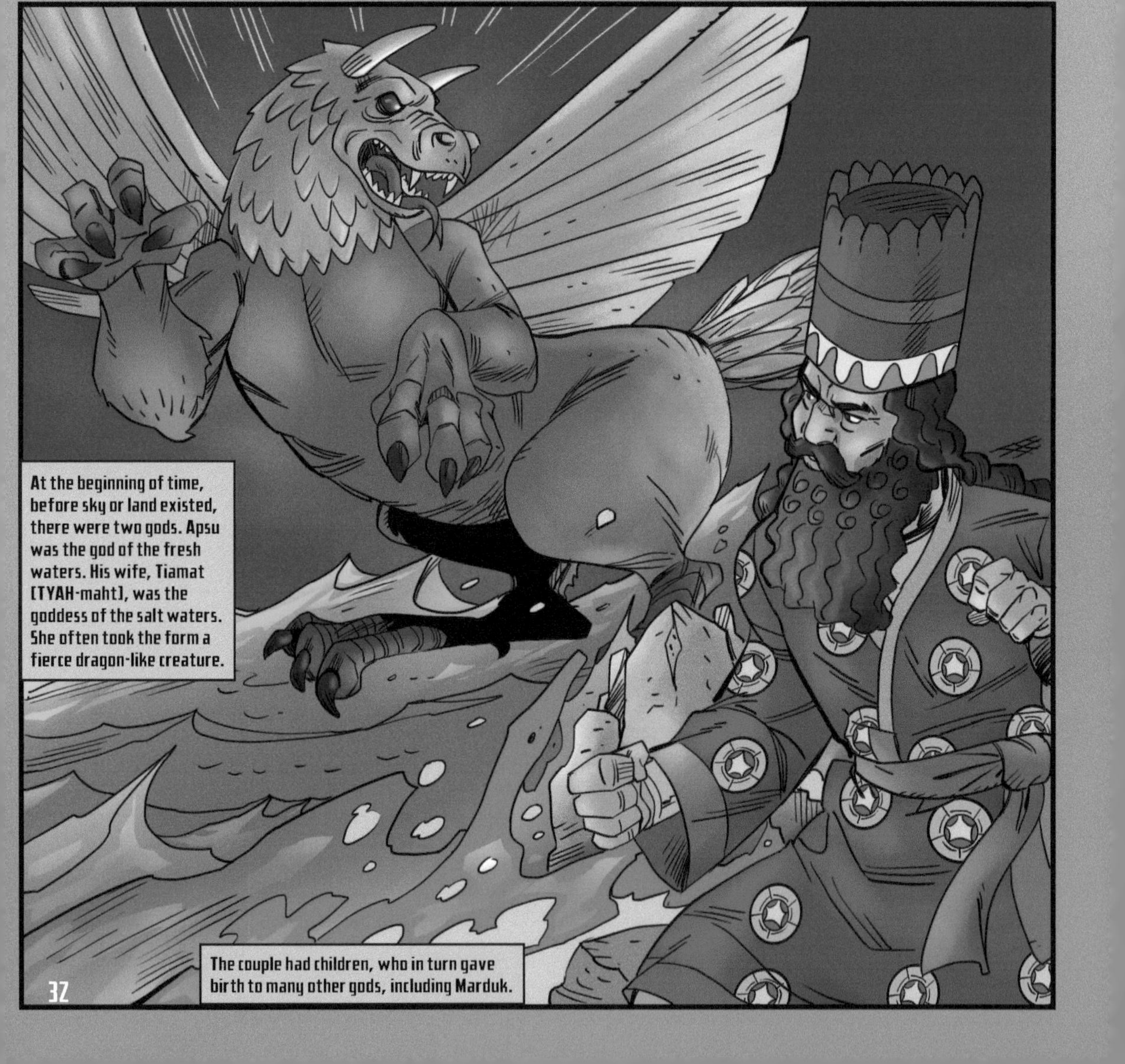
At the beginning of time, before sky or land existed, there were two gods. Apsu was the god of the fresh waters. His wife, Tiamat [TYAH-maht], was the goddess of the salt waters. She often took the form a fierce dragon-like creature.
The couple had children, who in turn gave birth to many other gods, including Marduk.

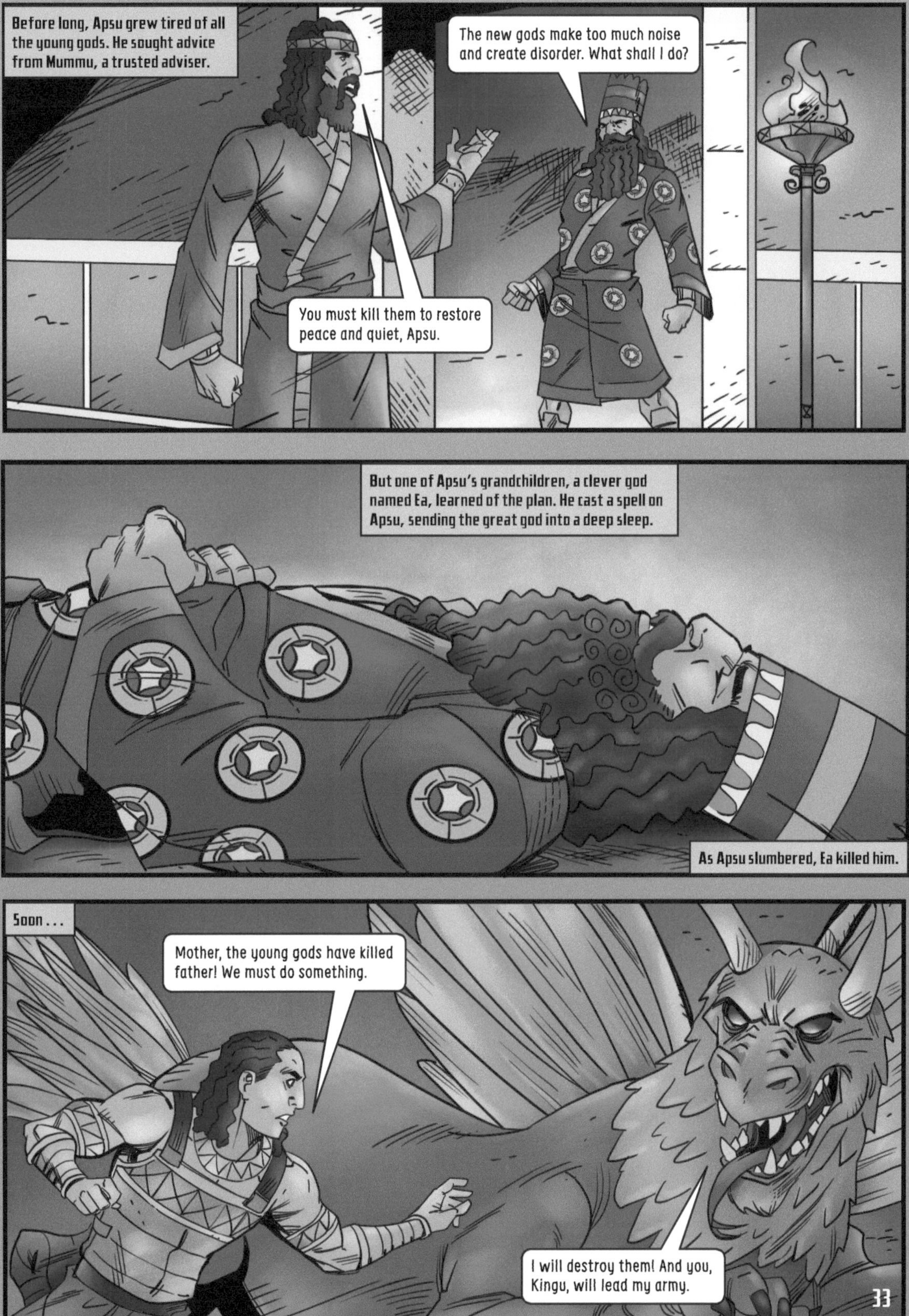

Before long, Apsu grew tired of all the young gods. He sought advice from Mummu, a trusted adviser.
The new gods make too much noise and create disorder. What shall I do?
You must kill them to restore peace and quiet, Apsu.
But one of Apsu's grandchildren, a clever god named Ea, learned of the plan. He cast a spell on Apsu, sending the great god into a deep sleep.
As Apsu slumbered, Ea killed him.
Soon . . .
Mother, the young gods have killed father! We must do something.
I will destroy them! And you, Kingu, will lead my army.

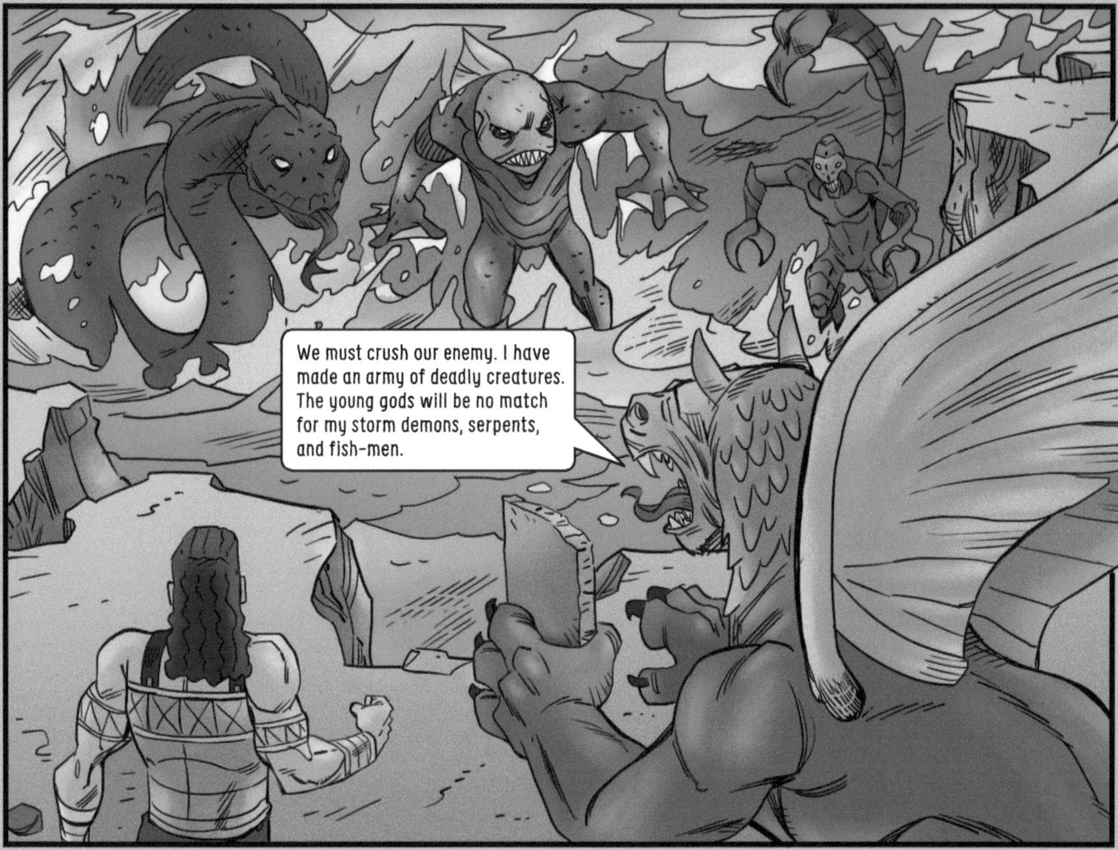
We must crush our enemy. I have made an army of deadly creatures. The young gods will be no match for my storm demons, serpents, and fish-men.

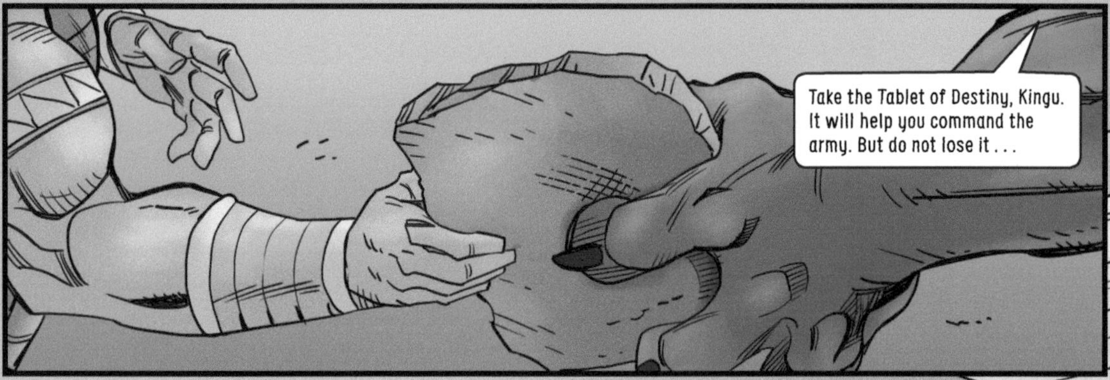
Take the Tablet of Destiny, Kingu. It will help you command the army. But do not lose it . . .

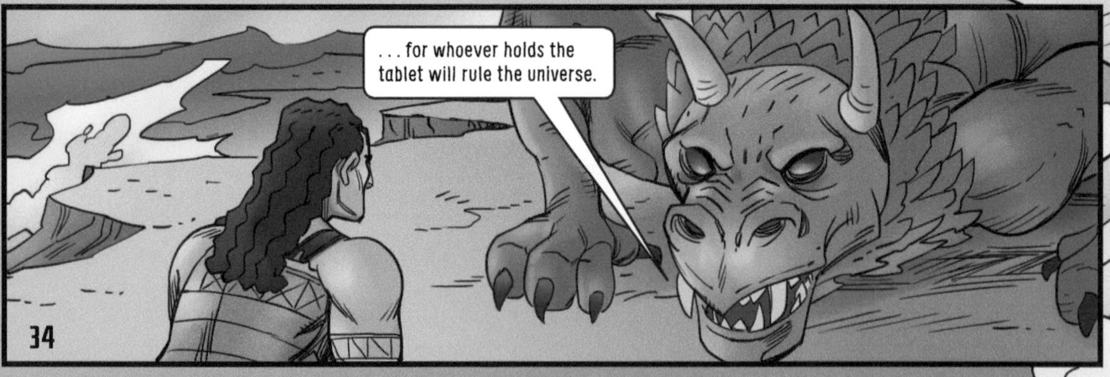
. . . for whoever holds the tablet will rule the universe.

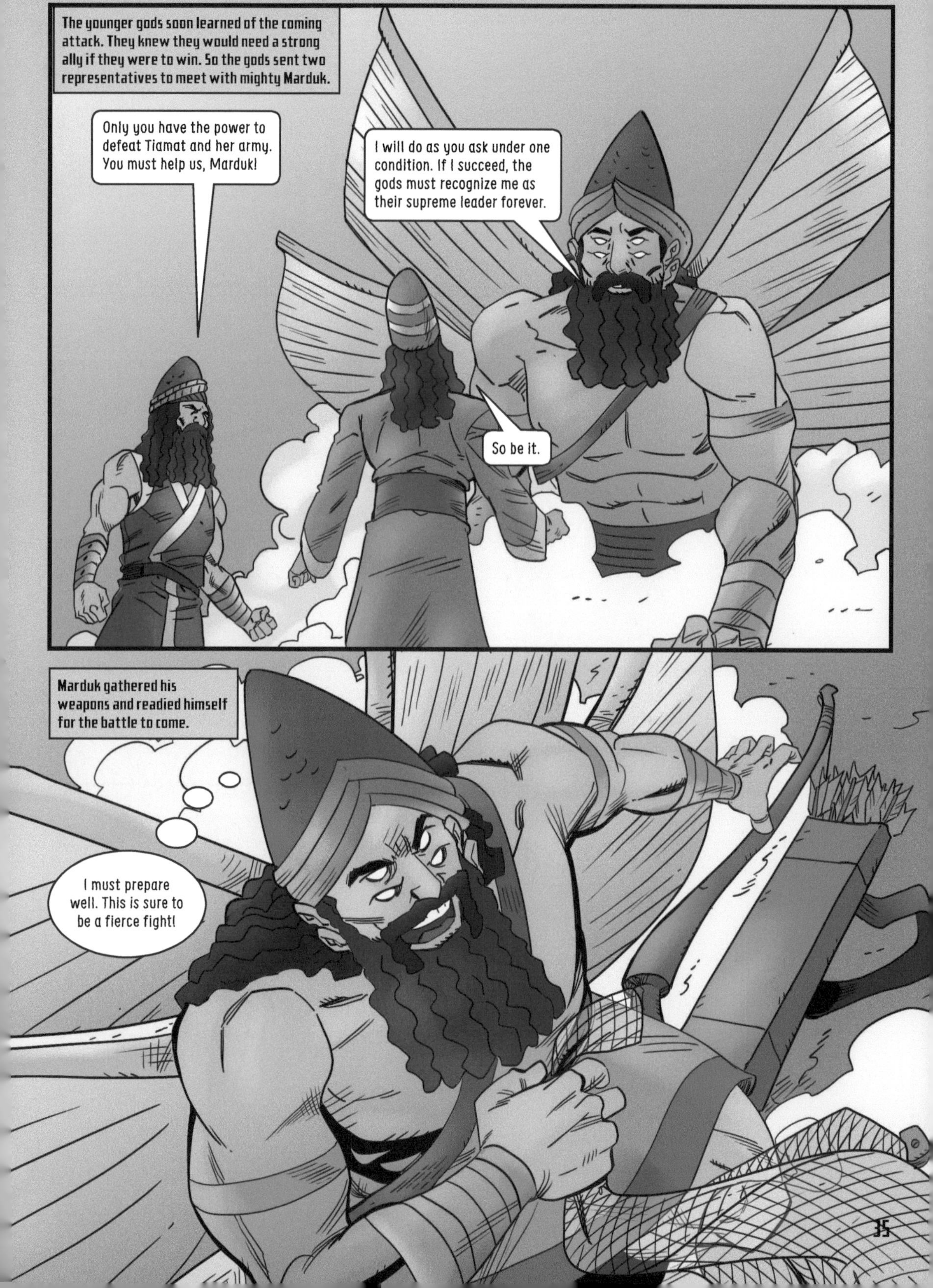
The younger gods soon learned of the coming attack. They knew they would need a strong ally if they were to win. So the gods sent two representatives to meet with mighty Marduk.
Only you have the power to defeat Tiamat and her army. You must help us, Marduk!
I will do as you ask under one condition. If I succeed, the gods must recognize me as their supreme leader forever.
So be it.
Marduk gathered his weapons and readied himself for the battle to come.
I must prepare well. This is sure to be a fierce fight!

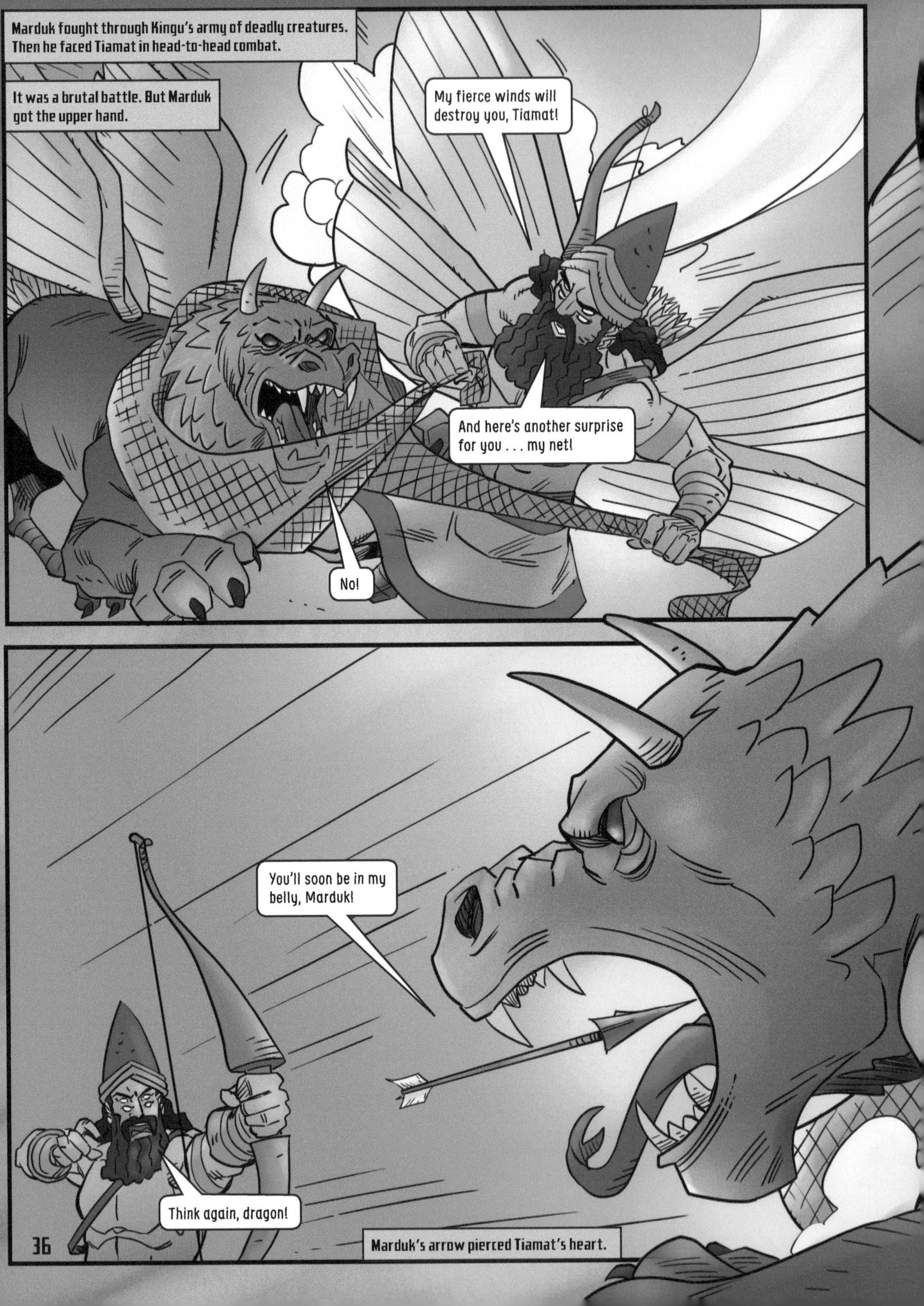
Marduk fought through Kingu's army of deadly creatures. Then he faced Tiamat in head-to-head combat.
It was a brutal battle. But Marduk got the upper hand.
My fierce winds will destroy you, Tiamat!
And here's another surprise for you . . . my net!
No!
You'll soon be in my belly, Marduk!
Think again, dragon!
Marduk's arrow pierced Tiamat's heart.

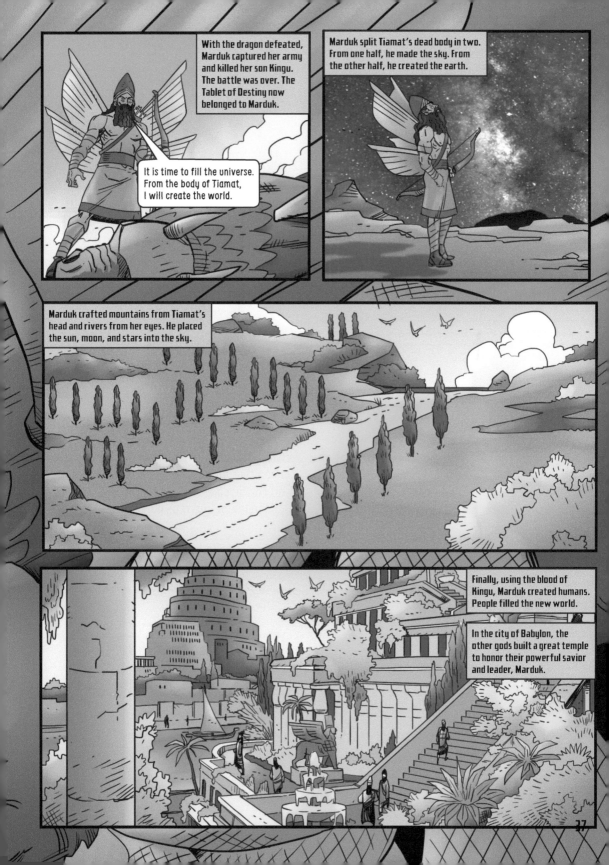

With the dragon defeated, Marduk captured her army and killed her son Kingu. The battle was over. The Tablet of Destiny now belonged to Marduk.

It is time to fill the universe. From the body of Tiamat, I will create the world.

Marduk split Tiamat's dead body in two. From one half, he made the sky. From the other half, he created the earth.

Marduk crafted mountains from Tiamat's head and rivers from her eyes. He placed the sun, moon, and stars into the sky.

Finally, using the blood of Kingu, Marduk created humans. People filled the new world.

In the city of Babylon, the other gods built a great temple to honor their powerful savior and leader, Marduk.

CHAPTER SEVEN

DAKUWAQA, THE FEARSOME SHARK GOD

A FIJIAN MYTH

ONE OF THE BEST-KNOWN GODS IN THE FIJI ISLANDS OF THE SOUTH PACIFIC OCEAN IS DAKUWAQA (DAH-KOO-**WAH**-KAH). THIS FEARLESS GOD COULD TAKE THE SHAPE OF A SHARK AND GUARDED THE REEF ENTRANCE TO THE ISLANDS. DAKUWAQA WAS ALSO ANGRY AND STUBBORN. HE OFTEN FOUGHT WITH OTHER GUARDIANS AND SEA CREATURES. BUT ONE DAY, HE FINALLY MET HIS MATCH.

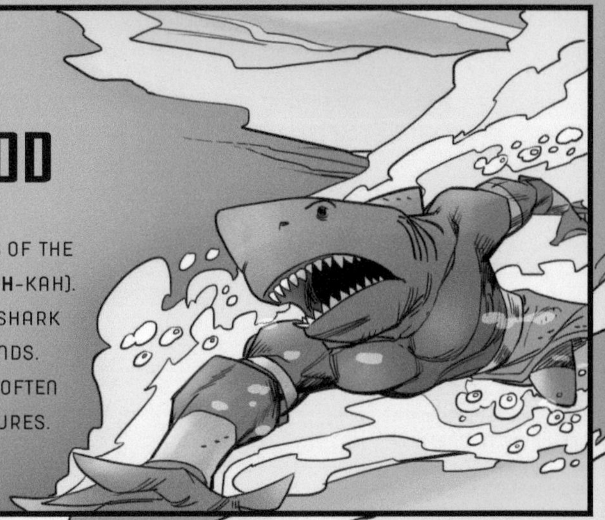

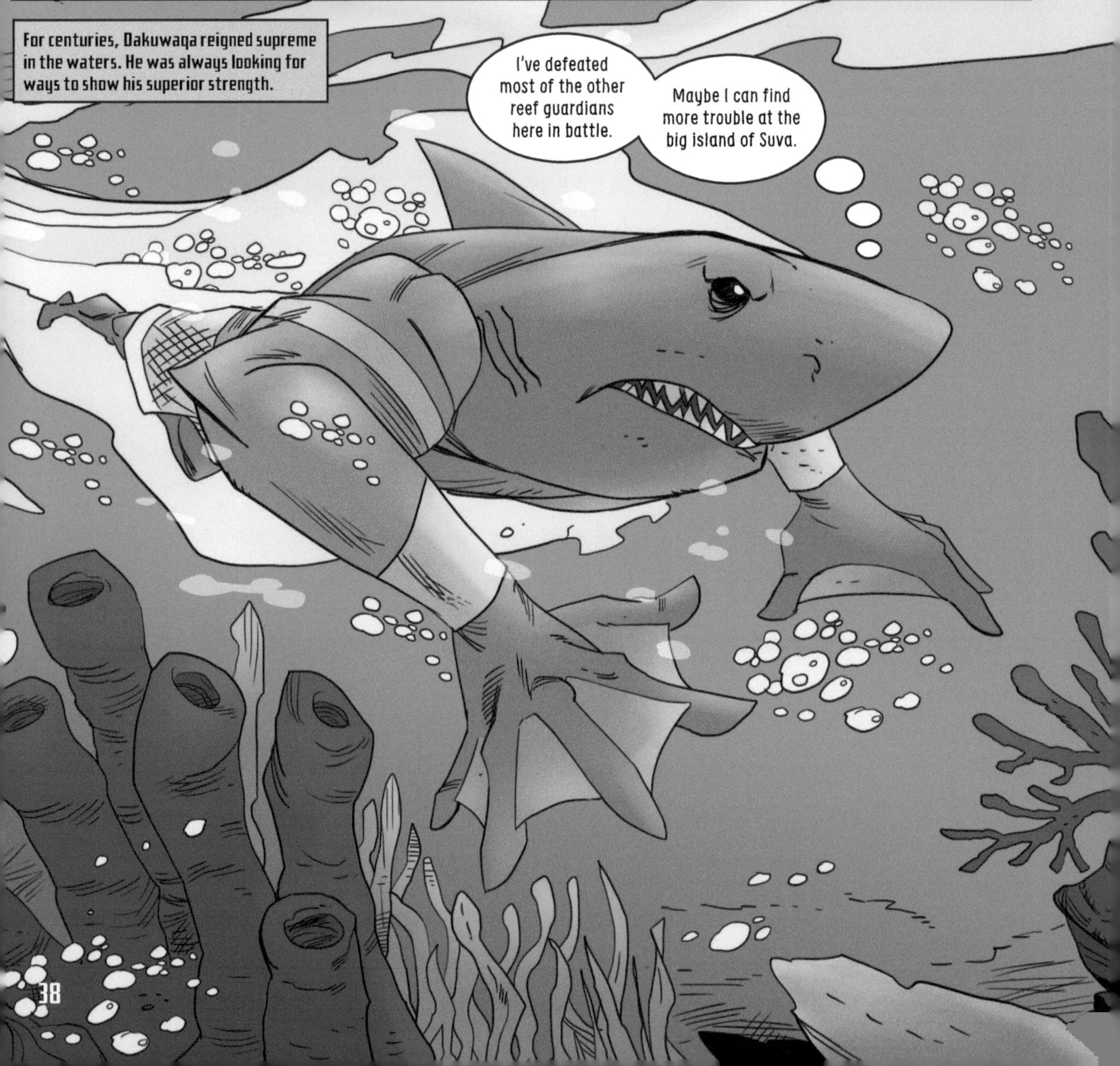
For centuries, Dakuwaqa reigned supreme in the waters. He was always looking for ways to show his superior strength.
I've defeated most of the other reef guardians here in battle.
Maybe I can find more trouble at the big island of Suva.

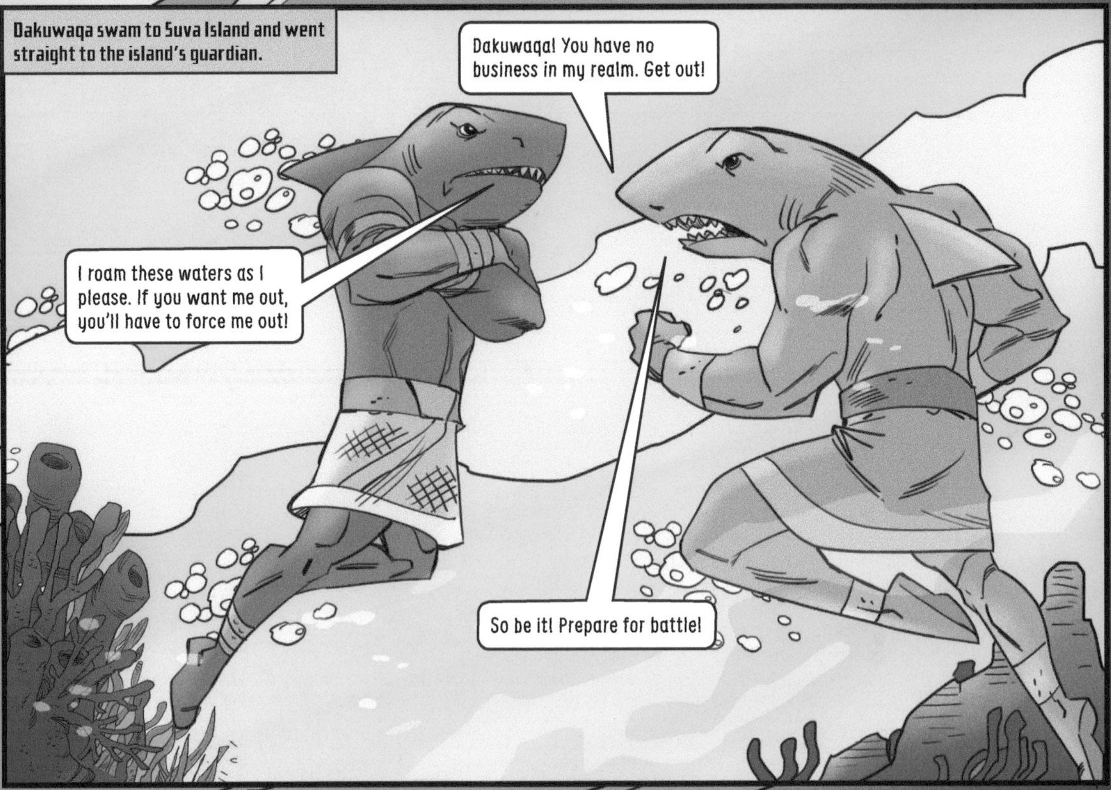
Dakuwaqa swam to Suva Island and went straight to the island's guardian.
Dakuwaqa! You have no business in my realm. Get out!
I roam these waters as I please. If you want me out, you'll have to force me out!
So be it! Prepare for battle!

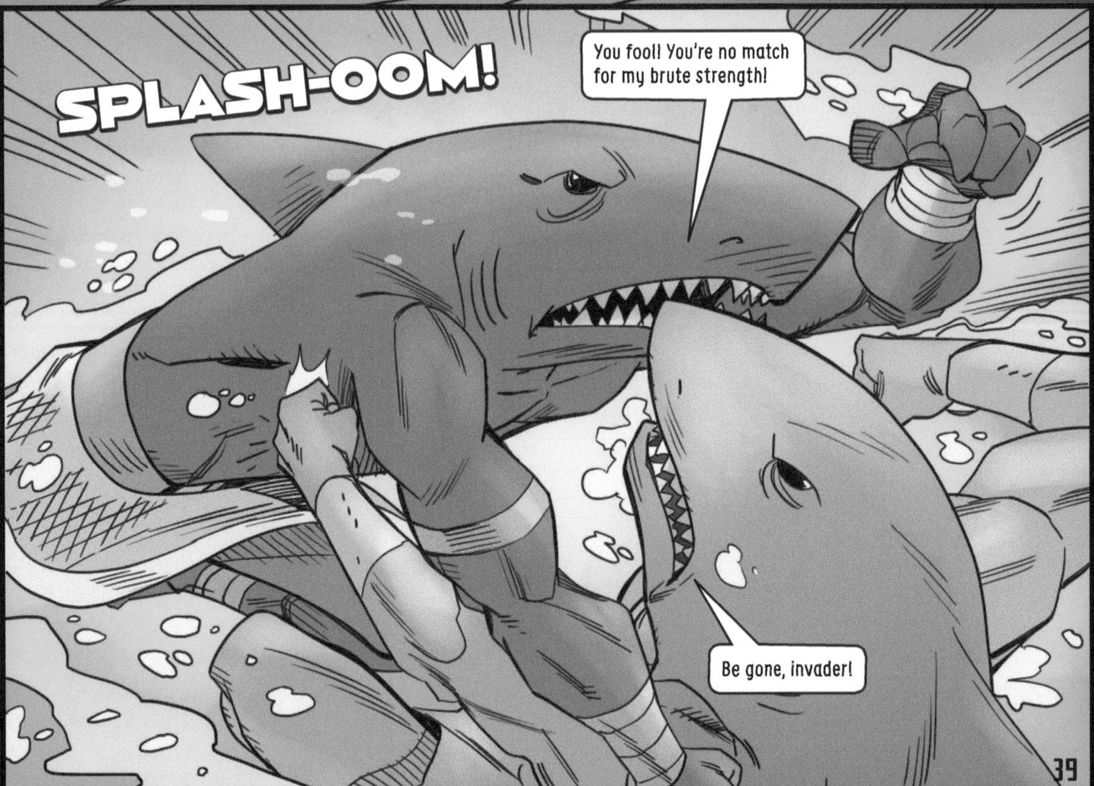
SPLASH-OOM!
You fool! You're no match for my brute strength!
Be gone, invader!

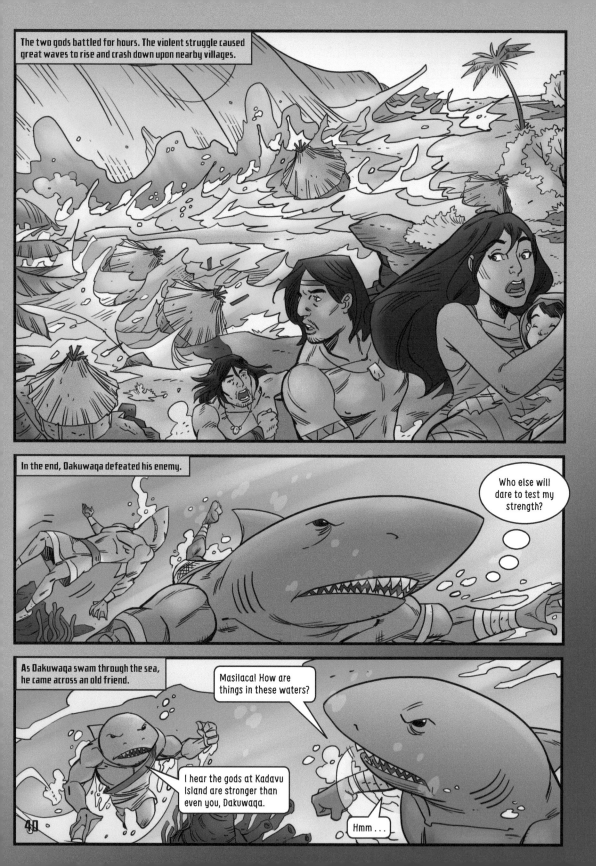

The two gods battled for hours. The violent struggle caused great waves to rise and crash down upon nearby villages.

In the end, Dakuwaqa defeated his enemy.

Who else will dare to test my strength?

As Dakuwaqa swam through the sea, he came across an old friend.

Masilaca! How are things in these waters?

I hear the gods at Kadavu Island are stronger than even you, Dakuwaqa.

Hmm . . .

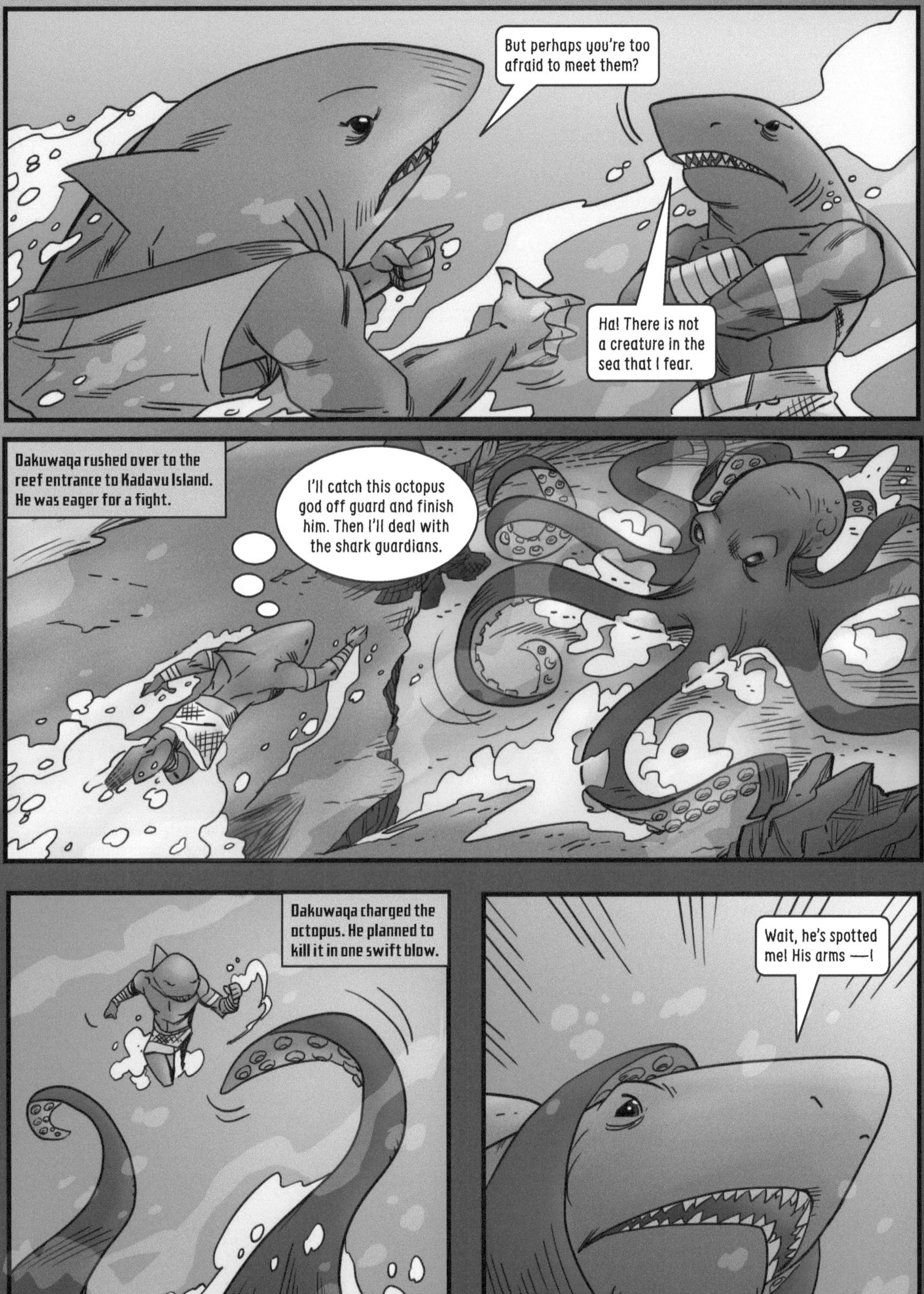
But perhaps you're too afraid to meet them?
Ha! There is not a creature in the sea that I fear.
Dakuwaqa rushed over to the reef entrance to Kadavu Island. He was eager for a fight.
I'll catch this octopus god off guard and finish him. Then I'll deal with the shark guardians.
Dakuwaqa charged the octopus. He planned to kill it in one swift blow.
Wait, he's spotted me! His arms —!
41

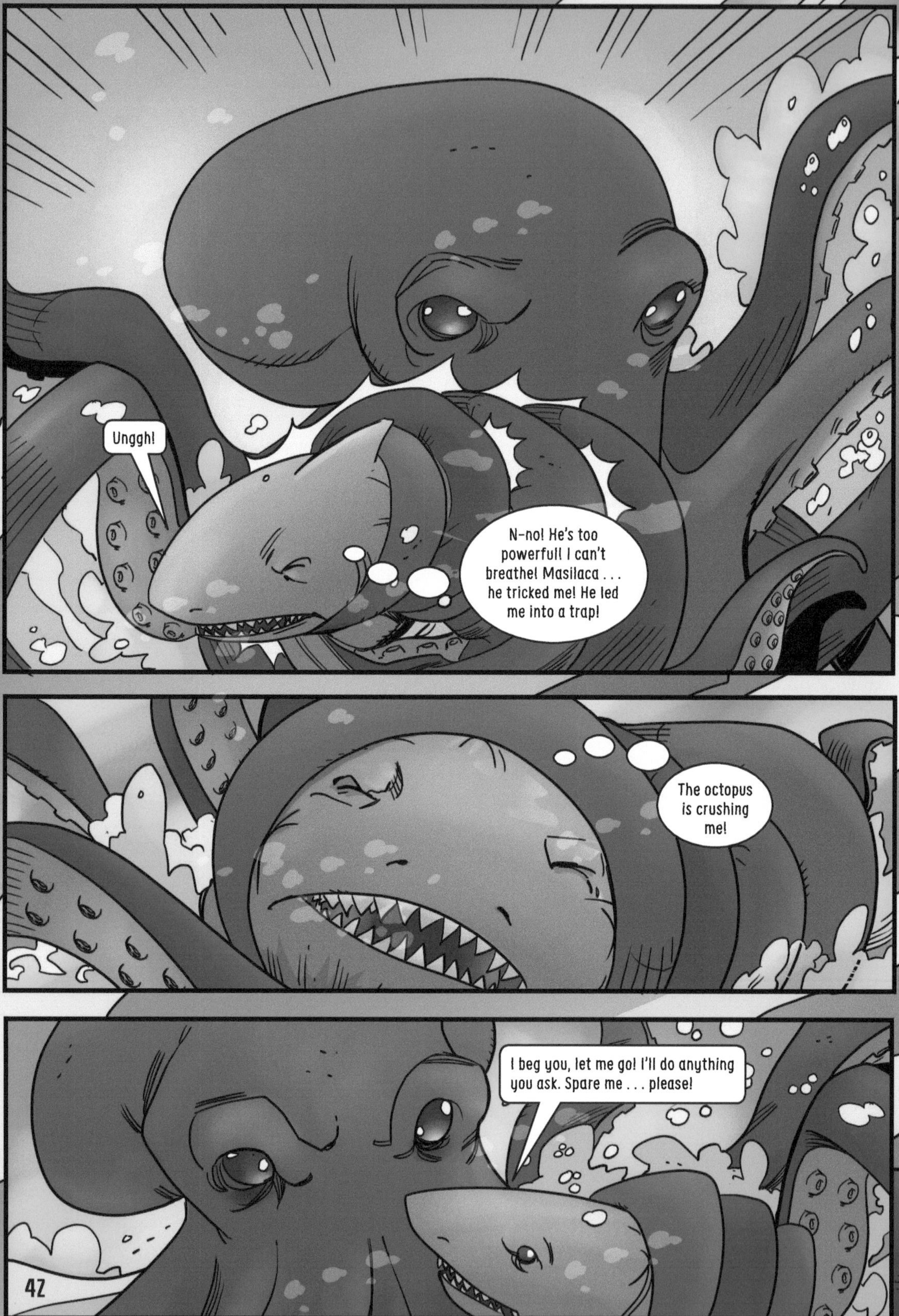
Ungghl
N-no! He's too powerful! I can't breathe! Masilaca . . . he tricked me! He led me into a trap!
The octopus is crushing me!
I beg you, let me go! I'll do anything you ask. Spare me . . . please!

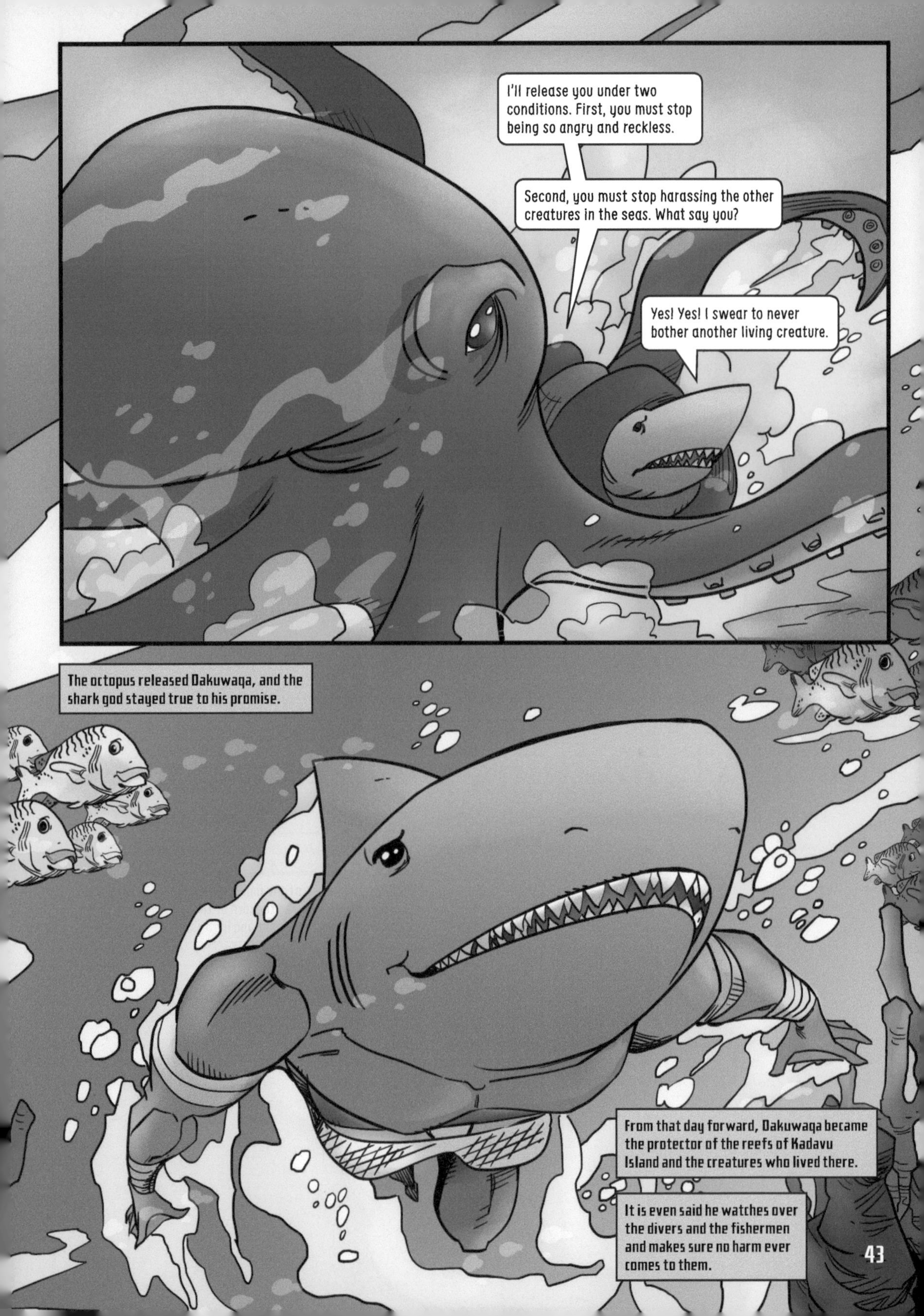
I'll release you under two conditions. First, you must stop being so angry and reckless.
Second, you must stop harassing the other creatures in the seas. What say you?
Yes! Yes! I swear to never bother another living creature.
The octopus released Dakuwaqa, and the shark god stayed true to his promise.
From that day forward, Dakuwaqa became the protector of the reefs of Kadavu Island and the creatures who lived there.
It is even said he watches over the divers and the fishermen and makes sure no harm ever comes to them.

MYTH MAP AND MORE

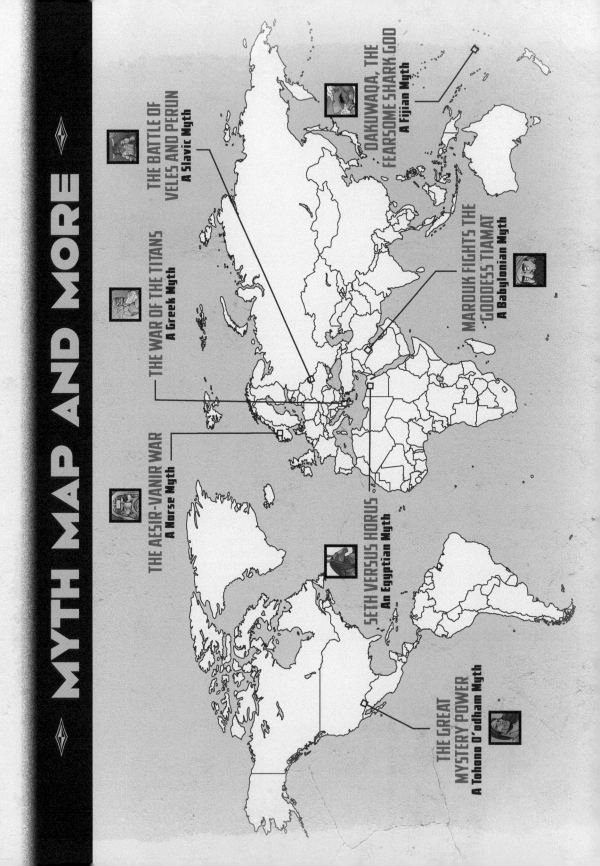

THE BATTLE OF
VELES AND PERUN
A Slavic Myth

DAKUWAQA, THE
FEARSOME SHARK GOD
A Fijian Myth

THE WAR OF THE TITANS
A Greek Myth

MARDUK FIGHTS THE
GODDESS TIAMAT
A Babylonian Myth

THE AESIR-VANIR WAR
A Norse Myth

SETH VERSUS HORUS
An Egyptian Myth

THE GREAT
MYSTERY POWER
A Tohono O'odham Myth

◇ The ten-year War of the Titans won by the Olympians is known by many different names. It's been called the Battle of the Gods and the Titan War. It's also referred to as Titanomachy, which is based on the Greek word *machy*, meaning "fighting" or "battling."

◇ Like most ancient peoples, the Egyptians worshipped many gods. The physical forms of the gods were often a combination of human and animal characteristics. Some gods and goddesses were depicted in more than one animal form. For example, the goddess Hathor has been shown as a woman with the head of a lion, a cow, and a cobra.

◇ To seal the truce after the Aesir-Vanir war, the two sides exchanged hostages. Njord and his children, Frey and Freya, went to live in Asgard. Njord and Frey were made priests, and Freya taught the Aesir the magic of her land. The Aesir sent the gods Honir and Mimir to live with the Vanir.

◇ In the city of Babylon, two great structures were built to honor the god Marduk. In the center of the city was an important temple complex called Esagila. Nearby was the towering temple Etemenanki. Built about 323 BC, Etemenanki stood 300 feet (90 meters) tall.

◇ Many myths were told long before they were written down. The method of passing on stories, beliefs, and histories through speaking instead of writing is called an oral tradition. This is why there are often slightly different versions of one myth. The story may have changed depending on who was telling it.

◇ In Japanese myths, the sun goddess Amaterasu often fights with her brother Susanoo, the storm god. In one story, Susanoo upsets his sister so much that she hides away in a cave, plunging the world into darkness. It is only after the other gods trick her into coming out that light is restored.

GLOSSARY

avenge (uh-VENJ)—to take revenge or satisfaction for

chaos (KAY-ohs)—complete and usually noisy disorder

domesticated (duh-MESS-tuh-kay-tuhd)—tamed; no longer wild

fertility (fur-TIHL-i-tee)—the condition of being able to have babies; the condition of soil being able to grow many plants

guardian (GAR-dee-uhn)—a person that protects or watches over someone or something

inheritance (in-HER-uh-tuhns)—the property, money, titles, and other things given to another person after the owner has died

nymph (NIMF)—a female spirit or goddess who may live in forests, meadows, or streams

pantheon (PAN-thee-on)—all the gods of a people

prophecy (PRAH-fuh-see)—a prediction about what will happen in the future

prosper (PROS-per)—to do very well or to be a success

reign (RAYN)—to rule as a king or queen

summon (SUHM-un)—to request or order that someone or something come or appear

READ MORE

Chambers, Catherine. *American Indian Stories and Legends.* All About Myths. Chicago: Raintree, 2014.

Gunderson, Jessica. *Olympians vs. Titans: An Interactive Mythological Adventure.* You Choose: Ancient Greek Myths. Mankato, Minn.: Capstone Press, 2017.

Krieg, Katherine. *What We Get from Norse Mythology.* Mythology and Culture. Ann Arbor, Mich.: Cherry Lake Publishing, 2015.

Staley, Erin. *Discovering Ancient Egypt.* Exploring Ancient Civilizations. New York: Rosen Education Service, 2015.

CRITICAL THINKING QUESTIONS

1. Seth and Horus battled for the right to rule Egypt. List the reasons why each god thought he should sit on the throne. Who would you pick to be pharaoh? Explain your choice using evidence from the story.
2. Now that you've read a few war myths, write your own myth about gods battling gods. Establish a plot, characters, settings, and a narrator to tell your story. Use descriptive words and phrases to draw the reader into your story.
3. Some myths, such as the stories about Marduk and Tiamat or Seth and Horus, have different versions. Use the Internet or visit your library to find other versions. Write a paragraph describing which details are the same and which are different. Why do you think there are multiple versions of the same story?

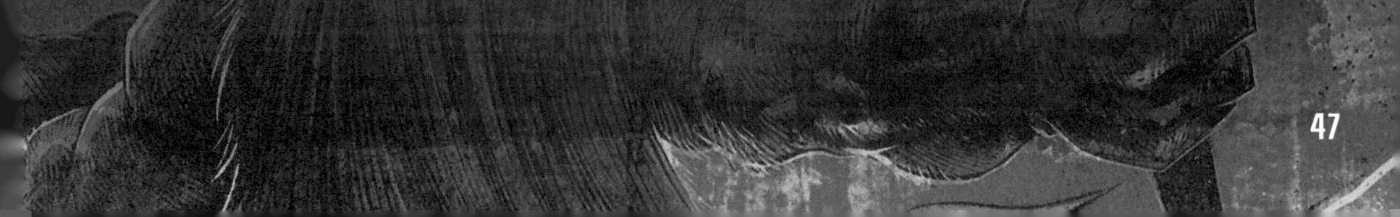

INTERNET SITES

Use FactHound to find Internet sites related to this book.

Visit *www.facthound.com*

Just type in 9781515766285 and go!

Super-cool stuff! Check out projects, games and lots more at
www.capstonekids.com

INDEX